Athletes of Iowa

Hometown Heroes

Athletes of Iowa

Hometown Heroes

Jim Simmelink

G and R Publishing
Waverly, Iowa

Athletes of Iowa: Hometown Heroes

G and R Publishing
507 Industrial Street
Waverly, IA 50677

International Standard Book Number:
ISBN 1-59971-550-3

Printed in the United States of America

For Information:

Iowa Hall of Pride
330 Park Street
Des Moines, Iowa 50309

Introduction

The impetus for this book came after I shared the Hometown Heroes print with a few friends; questions were asked about various athletes, everyone wanted to know from where each athlete hailed and what they had accomplished. After telling the stories a few times, I thought it would be easier if the information were in print. My intent in the final product was to provide a cross section of Iowa's finest athletes. Writing the book took much longer than I expected, but the work was enjoyable. Finding a new tidbit of information during the research process was similar to finding treasure.

I would like to thank Brian Thielges and Exchange State Bank of Adair and Winterset for providing financial support in the printing of the book. Thanks go to Tom Scott and his crew at G&R Publishing of Waverly for their help in printing and financing the book. For their help in proofing/editing this book, I wish to thank Marcia Meller of Centerville Community Schools and Sharon van Griethuysen of Adair-Casey Community Schools.

A special thank you must go to my family. My wife Delores and our children - Renee, Ryan, and Nicole - provided countless support during the completion of this project, each in their own special way.

Abbreviations used in the book

Baseball: 2B - Doubles, 3B - Triples, AB - At Bat. BA - Batting Average, ER - Earned Runs, ERA - Earned Run Average, G - Games, H - Hits, HR - Home Runs, IP - Innings Pitched, L - Loses, R - Runs, RBI - Runs Batted In, SV - Saves, W - Wins

Basketball: 3P - Three Point Goals, AST - Assists, BLK - Blocked Shots, FG -Field Goals, FT - Free Throws, G - Games, PTS - Points, RB - Rebounds, ST -Steals

Football: ATT - Attempts, AVG - Average BLK - Blocked, CMP - Completions, FF - Forced Fumble, FG - Field Goals, FGA - Field Goals Attempted, FR - Fumbles Recovered, G - Games, INT - Interceptions, KR - Kick Returns, NO - Number, PR - Punt Returns. PTS - Points, REC - Receptions, TD - Touchdowns, TKL - Tackles, SKS - Sacks, XPT - Extra Points, XPA - Extra Points Attempted, YDS - Yards

Hockey: GA - Goals Allowed, GP - Games Played, L - Loses, SV - Saves, SV% - Save Percentage, T - Ties, W – Wins

1 Lucille Robinson
2 Tom Brands
3 Terry Brands
4 Loren Meyer
5 Zeron Flemister
6 Willis Glassgow
7 Scott Clemmensen
8 Molly VanVenthuysen
9 Marvin Nelson
10 Randy Duncan
11 Mike Busch
12 George Saling
13 Jerry Reichow
14 Aubrey Devine
15 Jim Zalesky
16 Vern Den Herder
17 Bob Locker
18 Mark Kacmarynski
19 Juliana Korver
20 Joe Hatten
21 Denis Menke
22 Gerald Leeman
23 Mona Schallau
24 Beth Bader
25 Jerry Smith
26 Tom Hilgendorf
27 Mike Eischeid
28 A.G. Kruger
29 Brian Hansen
30 Dave Bancroft
31 Adam Timmerman
32 John Gregory
33 George Pipgras
34 Frank Gotch
35 Karlos Kirby
36 Glen Brand
37 Trev Alberts
38 Jared DeVries
39 Red Faber
40 Dedric Ward
41 Jack Dittmer
42 Kevin Kunnert
43 Bill Nelson
44 Al Couppee
45 Jamie Williams
46 Earl Whitehill
47 Buck Shaw
48 Natasha Kaiser
49 Dick Hoerner
50 Hank Severeid
51 Gary Thompson
52 Cap Anson
53 Don Perkins
54 Nick Collison
55 Reggie Roby
56 Jim Fanning
57 Jay Berwanger
58 Don Denkinger
59 Bobby Knoop
60 Kirk Hinrich
61 Morgan Taylor
62 Bob Oldis
63 Tiny Lund
64 Jim Doran
65 Dallas Clark
66 Brian Tietjens
67 Fred Hoiberg
68 Cal Eldred
69 Chad Hennings
70 Kurt Warner
71 Gene Baker
72 Raef LaFrentz

73 Mike Mercer
74 Martay Jenkins
75 Zoe Ann Olson
76 Judy Kimball
77 Bill Smith
78 Joey Woody
79 Bryce Paup
80 Kevin Little
81 Casey Blake
82 Bobby Hansen
83 Billy Cundiff
84 Mike Boddicker
85 Dan Gable
86 Marv Cook
87 Jay Hilgenberg
88 Joel Hilgenberg
89 Tavian Banks
90 Kenny Ploen
91 Murray Wier
92 Jon Lieber
93 Kip Janvrin
94 Johnny Lindell
95 Tom Farmer
96 Nile Kinnick
97 Bob Feller
98 Walt McCredie
99 Harris Coggeshall
100 Joe Laws
101 Dennis Gibson
102 Hal Trosky
103 Nate Kaeding
104 Wally Hilgenberg
105 Roger Craig
106 Casey Wiegmann
107 Stan Bahnsen
108 T.J. Rubley
109 Ed Podolak
110 Dazzy Vance
111 Fred Clarke
112 Matt Bullard
113 Zach Johnson
114 Don Norton
115 Lonnie Nielsen
116 Craig Oppel
117 Tim Dwight
118 Ricky Davis
119 Sage Rosenfels
120 Doreen Wilber
121 Al Feuerbach
122 Kent Ferguson
123 Mace Brown
124 Ross Verba
125 Elmer Layden
126 Ben Crain
127 Jeff Clement
128 Kyle Korver
129 Robert Gallery
130 Christine Thorburn
131 Duke Slater
132 Keith Molesworth
133 Jim Kelly
134 Debbie Esser
135 Corkey Nydle
136 Bing Miller
137 Eddie Watt
138 Bob Allen
139 Jack Fleck
140 Bill Koll
141 Kevin Ritz
142 James Jones
143 Denise Long
144 Tony Baker

1 – Lucille Robinson

Hometown: Des Moines

This Hall of Fame golfer was born in Ottumwa in 1911. She began her schooling in Eldon, and then in 1918 her father moved the family to Des Moines when he entered the insurance business. The children of the neighborhood were predominately boys so Lucille hung around them. One of their favorite activities was going to the local country club at dawn to play golf until they had to leave the course at ten o'clock.

At twelve years of age she entered the City Women's Tournament, scoring well enough to make the championship flight. It didn't take many tries to win the championship when three years later she topped the field to take her first title. She was fifteen at the time of her victory, still a student at Roosevelt High School. Since there was not a high school golf program for girls, the city tournaments were her only place for competition. While a student at Drake University, Lucille won four additional city titles.

The summer following her graduation from Roosevelt, Robinson won the first of five Iowa state championships. In addition to her five Iowa titles she won three in Wisconsin and five in Nebraska. Her five Iowa titles came in a six-year span. The year following her first win she was the runner-up, then reeled off four straight championships.

After graduating from Drake, Lucille burst on to the national golf scene with an impressive win at the Women's Western Amateur. One must remember this was 1933, long before the advent of an established professional tour. The Western was one of the country's top tournaments, and with her victory she earned a spot on the victorious 1934 United States Curtis Cup team. Winning the South Atlantic in 1936 garnered her an invitation to a second Curtis team, but she declined in favor of marriage. The couple moved to Wisconsin, and while winning state championships she finished her national play with a flare, winning both the Western Amateur and the Trans-Mississippi in 1941.

When her husband returned from military service, the couple relocated to Nebraska where Lucille became involved in their state golf tournaments. As a way of giving back to golf, she served many years on the Trans-Mississippi Golf Association board of directors to help direct that annual event.

2 – Tom Brands

Hometown: Sheldon

Tom was one of the most intense competitors the wrestling world has seen. As youngsters, a family friend steered Tom and his twin brother Terry toward wrestling after it was apparent that basketball would not be their sport. Wrestling at Sheldon High School, he qualified twice for the state tournament, winning one title. Iowa coach Dan Gable saw potential, recruiting Tom to the Iowa Hawkeye program.

A four time All-American, Tom claimed three individual NCAA championships, including Outstanding Wrestler recognition at the 1992 meet. His Hawkeye career record of 158-7-2 includes an undefeated season in 1991, with a 45-0 record.

After graduation from Iowa, Tom stayed in shape and continued to wrestle competitively, winning a gold medal at the 1993 World Freestyle Championships. He and Terry were named 1993 Co-USA Wrestling Athlete of the Year and 1993 Amateur Wrestling News Man of the Year. Between 1993 and 1996, he was the top United States wrestler in his weight class and represented the United States in major international events. Competing in the 136.5-pound class in the 1996 Olympics, Tom overwhelmed his opponents, winning his four matches en route to the gold medal by outscoring them nineteen to one.

Serving as an assistant coach at Iowa, Tom helped the Hawkeyes win seven NCAA championships. In 2000 he was named the National Wrestling Coaches Association Assistant Coach of the Year. He served as an assistant coach for the 2002 and 2003 U.S. Freestyle World Teams, and both years was named Freestyle Coach of the Year by USA Wrestling. Tom was one of three coaches for the U.S. Olympic Team at the 2004 Athens Games.

After serving twelve years as an assistant, Tom was hired as the head coach at Virginia Tech in 2004, making an immediate impact on the program in his first season. He led the Hokies to an Atlantic Coast Conference dual meet title, a school record for dual meet wins, and had a school record five wrestlers qualify for the NCAA Championships. In April of 2006 Tom resigned as Tech's coach when he was selected to succeed Jim Zalesky as the head coach at the University of Iowa.

3 – Terry Brands

Hometown: Sheldon

In April of 2005, USA Wrestling hired Terry Brands as its National Freestyle Resident Coach. Working closely with National Freestyle Coach and former Iowa State wrestler Kevin Jackson at the Olympic Training Center, Brands trains the nation's elite wrestlers as they prepare for international and Olympic competitions.

One of the nation's great freestyle wrestlers, Terry has extensive international wrestling experience. He was a two-time World Cup champion and won a gold medal at the 1995 Pan-American Games. He was a member of two U.S. teams to win World Team Freestyle Titles. Twice he won a silver medal in the Yarygin Tournament held in Krasnoyarsk, Russia. Brands qualified for the 1997 and 1999 U.S. World Wrestling Teams, but could not compete due to injury.

In 1996 both Terry and Tom had aspirations of winning a gold medal at the Olympic games held in Atlanta. Tom earned a spot on the team at 136.5 pounds, while Terry lost a best-of-three finals match to Kendall Cross. Tom and Kendall went on to win gold and Terry was left with an empty feeling. Staging a comeback following an injury, he earned a spot on the 2000 team and won a bronze medal at the Olympic games in Sydney, Australia.

Known as one of the sport's top technicians, Terry has experienced success as a coach. From 1992 through 2000 he served as an assistant at the University of Iowa with Dan Gable and Jim Zalesky. He also had stints at Nebraska and NAIA-power Montana State-Northern. In 2002 Brands was hired as the head coach at the University of Tennessee - Chattanooga. During his three years at the helm, the program came to national prominence. His squad won the 2005 Southern Conference Championship and had two wrestlers earn All-American recognition.

As a Hawkeye wrestler, he completed his career with a 137-7 record, won three Big Ten titles, earned a NCAA runner-up in finish 1991, and won NCAA championships in 1990 and 1992. As a wrestler for Sheldon High School, he wrestled in three finals at the state tournament, winning two state titles.

4 – Loren Meyer

Hometown: Ruthven

Standing 6'10" Loren Meyer was a force in basketball for Ruthven-Ayrshire High School. He displayed his athletic ability in a game against Mallard during his junior year. During one team possession he canned a jumper from the top of the key. When the defender came out the next time to take away the shot, Meyer pump faked and drove to the basket for a dunk. Loren continued that type of dominant play, earning first team All-State recognition following his junior and senior seasons.

Heavily recruited, Loren chose to play for Johnny Orr at Iowa State. His play during the first two seasons could be categorized as the learning process needed when going from small high school basketball to Division I basketball. As a junior he was off to a great start, leading the team in scoring and rebounding through twelve games. Then in January of 1994 a train hit the truck in which he was riding. Suffering a broken collarbone, he missed the remainder of the season. Making a successful return for the 1994-95 season, Meyer became an honorable mention All-Big Eight selection.

Selected by the Dallas Mavericks in the first round of the 1995 NBA draft, Loren started twenty-one games in his rookie season. Midway through his second season he was traded to the Phoenix Suns, playing in a total of fifty-four games with thirty-three starts for the two clubs. After spending all of 1997-98 on the injured list while recovering from lumbar spine surgery, Meyer appeared in fourteen games for the Denver Nuggets during his final NBA season.

Loren finished his professional career playing with the Chester Jets of the British Basketball League. The team was one of the league's best and Meyer led them in scoring. He was selected to the mid-season All-Star game and at season's end chosen the league's Player of the Year.

NBA Record

3 Seasons	G	FG	3P	FT	RB	AST	PTS
Career	140	260	8	117	480	77	645

5 – Zeron Flemister

Hometown: Sioux City

Flemister was born in Chicago, but his family moved to Sioux City when he was a youngster. A gifted athlete, Zeron became a three-sport star at West High School. A sprinter on the track team, he helped the 400-meter relay team win a state championship. The Black Raider basketball team did not compete for championships, but Flemister's skills shone as he earned first team All-State honors. There was a time when he thought basketball would be his ticket to college; instead it was football that brought him to the University of Iowa. As a three-year starter at running back for West, he set the city game-rushing record with 327 yards and six touchdowns performance while playing only the first half of a blowout victory.

After a red-shirt season for Iowa in 1995, Zeron saw limited action as a tight end and on special teams his freshman season. Sitting out his sophomore season due to personal problems, he came back as a junior to catch five passes. As a senior he started seven games before playing in three postseason all-star games. Zeron is the first person in his family to earn a college degree, an accomplishment in which he takes pride.

Flemister signed with the Washington Redskins as a rookie free agent in 2000. During his four seasons in Washington he was a part time starter, catching a total of thirty-eight passes. As an unrestricted free agent in 2004 he signed with the New England Patriots, hoping for a trip to the Super Bowl. A week into training camp he tore an Achilles tendon and missed the entire season. There was some thought that the injury would be career ending, but Zeron resumed his career as a tight end with the Oakland Raiders. Used primarily as an extra blocker on running plays, he made three starts while playing in twelve games of the 2005 season.

NFL Receiving Record

4 Seasons	G	REC	YDS	TD
Career	60	38	439	4

6 – Willis Glassgow

Hometown: Shenandoah

Who scored the first touchdown in Kinnick Stadium? Willis Glassgow in 1929. Voted as a defensive back to the all-time University of Iowa team by the fans, Glassgow was a first team All-American in 1929 after a second team berth the previous year. Willis capped off a brilliant career by being named the Big Ten's MVP, the first time for a Hawkeye. He first attended the University of Nebraska to play football. Lincoln is closer to Glassgow's hometown of Shenandoah than Iowa City and Willis decided to try his luck with the Cornhuskers. Nebraska was looking for size in their running backs and not the speed that Willis used to earn first team All-State quarterback honors in 1922. Instead of serving as a backup at Nebraska, he decided to transfer to Iowa.

After sitting out the 1926 season, Willis made a big splash in his Hawk debut. He scored three touchdowns and kicked two extra points, all in the second quarter. His abilities helped Iowa win important games, none more than a couple of wins over the powerful Minnesota teams of that time. He capped his collegiate career by playing in the 1930 East/West Shrine Bowl.

Multi-talented, Willis played two professional sports following his Hawkeye days. In 1930 Glassgow played football for Portsmouth, then during the 1931 season he was with the football Cardinals of Chicago. Good enough to letter three years for the Iowa baseball team, he signed with the St. Louis Cardinals after his football years. He played one season with St. Joseph in the Western League.

Using the money he earned from the professional sports, Willis put himself through law school. After graduation he began a practice in Shenandoah, where he became Page County attorney. In 1959 at age 52, Willis died after being stricken with leukemia, long before his induction into the Iowa Sports Hall of Fame in1973.

NFL Game Record

1930 Port: 12 G, Pass 1 TD, Rush 3TD, KR **1** TD, 4 XP, 28 Pts
1931 ChiC: 9 G

7 – Scott Clemmensen

Hometown: Urbandale

Hockey has gained recent popularity in Iowa. The first native Iowan to play in the National Hockey League is Scott Clemmensen. Scott was born in Des Moines and took up hockey at a young age. He played on travel teams based in Des Moines, then as a freshman played for the Valley-Dowling (later called Des Moines Capitals) high school team that won the state championship. Scott earned first team All-State honors as a goal tender from the Iowa High School Hockey League in his sophomore and junior years. An honor student at Urbandale High School, he also played football for two seasons before concentrating on hockey.

Instead of playing high school hockey his senior year, Scott played for the Des Moines Buccaneers of the USHL. He tended goal for twenty games in 1995-96, winning ten. He also played the 1996-97 season for the Bucs, finishing with a 22-9-2 record and was selected to participate in the 1997 USHL All-Star Game. Scott won the Bob Punsalam Contribution to Amateur Hockey Award in both 1996 and 1997.

Selected by the New Jersey Devils in the eighth round of the 1997 National Hockey League entry draft, Scott instead chose to attend Boston College. Starting as a freshman, he was named to the Hockey East All-Rookie team. In his senior season he recorded thirty wins, a career high, and led the BC team to the NCAA championship. Scott was named to the All-Tournament Team and received honorable mention recognition by Hockey East.

Beginning his professional career in 2001 with the Devils top minor league team in Albany, he appeared in two NHL games later that season. As a last-minute substitution, Scott made his first NHL start in January of 2004. He played well, gaining his first win by shutting out the Pittsburgh Penguins.

NHL Record

Year	Team	GP	W	L	T	GA	SV	SV%
2001-02	New Jersey	2	0	0	0	1	5	.800
2003-04	New Jersey	4	3	1	0	4	84	.952
2005-06	New Jersey	13	3	4	0	40	260	.881
Career		19	6	5	0	45	344	.896

8 – Molly VanVenthuysen

Hometown: Moravia

Monna Lea VanVenthuysen is better known by one of sport's great nicknames, "Machine Gun Molly Bolin." Born in Canada, Molly was raised in Moravia after moving to Iowa as a fifth grade student. She began playing basketball in junior high, but her big splash came in the first game of her junior season when she scored sixty-three points. Five times during her career for the Moravia Mohawkettes she scored more than seventy points. She was selected as a high school All-American and was invited to try out for both the Pan-American team and 1976 Olympic Basketball Team.

During the two years she played at Grand View College she adapted well to the five-player college game, setting many Grand View scoring records. She was married while at Grand View, becoming Molly Bolin.

In 1978 Bolin was the first player to sign with the Iowa Cornets of the newly formed Women's Basketball League. Once she became acclimated to the professional game, she blossomed into one of the league's stars. While playing for the Cornets, Molly was tabbed "Machine Gun" because of her uncanny ability to score in bursts. She is the league's career scoring leader, the leader in game points scored, had the highest season points per game average, scored the four highest game point totals, was voted league MVP, and was named All-Pro each year of the league's existence.

In the summer of 1984 she was on an All-Star Team that played exhibition games to prepare the U.S. Women's Basketball Team for Olympic competition. Later that year she played for the Columbus Minks of the Women's American Basketball Association (WABA). During the league's only season, Molly was featured in *Sports Illustrated* and on NBC's *Sports World.*

When her professional career ended in 1984 Molly continued to promote women's basketball and conducted clinics. She was hired to produce a women's pro basketball, three-on-three tournament and shortly following the WNBA was formed. Bolin was inducted into the Iowa High School Basketball Hall of Fame in 1986 and the Grandview College Athletic Hall of Fame in 1999.

9 – Marvin Nelson

Hometown: Fort Dodge

In the 1930s long distance, or marathon swimming, was a very popular spectator sport. In 1933 an estimated 100,000 people attended the Canadian National Exhibition Marathon Swim at Toronto, many to see Marvin "Duke" Nelson. During a five-year span Nelson was the world's premier distance swimmer. He won multiple national and international races, most fifteen miles in length. In 1979 he was enshrined in the International Marathon Swimmers Hall of Fame.

Born and raised in Fort Dodge, Duke participated as a member of the Dodger basketball team and ran the half-mile on the track team. However, it was swimming that became his passion, as he would swim endlessly in the pool at the YMCA. A couple of the Y's directors took notice, coaxing Nelson to enter a competition against some of the world's best swimmers. In 1928 he entered the Canadian National in Toronto, managing to complete only half the distance. Again in 1929 he failed to finish, this time only fifty yards from the finish and in second place at the time. The culprit in these races was deemed the icy cold waters of Lake Ontario.

The trio hatched a plan to use the elements of Iowa as part of a training routine. Earlier Nelson had trained during summers at Lake Okoboji and the Des Moines River in Fort Dodge. Now he would continue to swim in the river throughout autumn and into the winter, even when ice formed. At times the ice was so thick they had to use machines to cut blocks to be removed. When the 1930 Canadian National race was complete, Marvin Nelson was the winner, a world champion at the age of nineteen.

In 1933 Duke became the first two-time winner in Toronto and the following year added a third championship. Marvin furthered his legend with a pair of wins at the Century of Progress fair in Chicago during a time when he was unbeatable.

Nelson was at the top of his game and he had a plan to cash in on his fame. He bet all takers he could complete a never accomplished swim, crossing the English Channel and back. He put up $25,000 versus odds of fifty to one. With the outbreak of World War II he never had the chance to attempt the fete, ending his competitive swimming.

10 – Randy Duncan

Hometown: Des Moines

Randy Duncan was born in Osage, lived a short time in Mason City, and then moved to Des Moines while in grade school. His high school career was spent at Roosevelt High School as a two-sport all-state performer. A first team guard on the basketball team that finished as the state tournament runner-up, Randy was more heavily recruited as a quarterback. After leading Roosevelt to an undefeated football season in 1954, it appeared he would join friends to attend the University of Colorado, but instead chose the University of Iowa due to his respect for assistant coach Bump Elliott.

As a mid-year graduate from Roosevelt, Randy spent two spring practices and a fall season before becoming eligible to play. This was the era of two-way players, he was a quarterback on offense and played safety on defense. Playing the majority of his college career before the use of facemasks, he broke his nose eight times while playing at Iowa, most often tackling the ball carrier.

After serving as Kenny Ploen's backup as a sophomore, Duncan was named the starter in 1957, leading the team to 7-1-1 record. As a senior he guided a talented Iowa squad to a Big Ten championship and a Rose Bowl victory. The Hawkeye offense was the nation's leader in total offense and Randy led in completion percentage and passing yardage. He was named first team All-Conference, the 1958 Big Ten MVP, and selected as a first team All-American. The runner-up in the 1958 Heisman Trophy balloting, Duncan won the Walter Camp player of the year award and the award he most cherished, Iowa MVP as voted by his teammates. In 1997 Randy was honored with enshrinement into the College Football Hall of Fame

Selected by the Green Bay Packers with the first pick of the 1959 NFL draft, Randy instead signed with the British Columbia Lions of the CFL. That was before Vince Lombardi coached in Green Bay and the Lions offered more money. After two seasons in Canada with mixed success, Randy did not return because he began law school at Drake. He found he could sign with the Dallas Texans and attend law classes at Southern Methodist University. Spending most of the season on the bench, Duncan retired to complete a law degree at Drake.

11 – Mike Busch

Hometown: Donahue

When Mike Busch completed his collegiate eligibility in the spring of 1990 he had to decide whether to pursue a professional career in baseball or football. There wasn't a need to decide at North Scott High School, he was able to play both sports. Busch was a first-team All-State selection as a tight end during his senior football season after being a third-team pick as a junior. He was the team's MVP for three consecutive years. Additionally a three-year starter in baseball, Mike set the school record for home runs in a career.

At Iowa State he again played football and baseball. On the gridiron he was a four-year letter-winner and first-team All-American. In baseball he held school records for most home runs in a season and during a career. He was honored as the team's MVP his senior season, earned the MVP award in the Big Eight Conference tournament, and was selected for All-American honors. For his accomplishments he was voted as the Big Eight Male Athlete of the Year.

Mike had to decide between the two sports in 1990 when he was selected by Tampa Bay in the NFL draft and by the L.A. Dodgers in the amateur draft; he chose baseball. After four years in the minors, Mike had an opportunity to play for the Dodgers as a replacement player in 1995. He played, raising the ire of regular players and while he played thirty-eight games in 1996 he was an outcast that was sent back to the minor league. The Cleveland Indians signed Mike in 1997, but failing to make the team he headed for the Northern League.

The Northern League is an independent league and Mike spent time playing with teams in Sioux Falls and Fargo. In 2002 he became the hitting coach for the Lincoln Saltdogs and after three seasons was hired as the manager of the Calgary Vipers. Mike was selected to manage the league's north division team in the 2005 All-Star game.

Major League Hitting Record

Year	Team	G	AB	R	H	2B	3B	HR	RBI	BA
1995	LAD	13	17	3	4	0	0	3	6	.235
1996	LAD	38	83	8	18	4	0	4	17	.217
Career		51	100	11	22	4	0	7	23	.220

12 – George Saling

Hometown: Corydon

Saling grew up in the Wayne County area attending Corydon High School. Getting top notch coaching from George Bresnahan while attending the University of Iowa, George developed himself into a world-class hurdler. The first indication of things to come happened in 1930 at the Texas Relays when he ran a 24.0 time in the low hurdles.

His most memorable year came during his senior season in 1932. It began at the Kansas Relays where he won the high hurdles in 14.6 seconds. At the Drake Relays he lowered that time to 14.4, establishing a new Relays record. As the Big Ten Conference meet approached, it was evident that George and Ohio State hurdler Jack Keller were heading to a showdown. Keller edged Saling in the highs for the win, but George came back in the lows with a spectacular time of 23.0 to claim victory. At the NCAA Championships the outcome of the highs was reversed as Saling took the win. George's winning time of 14.1 smashed the world record time, but only went into the books as the NCAA best. Their personal hurdle duel continued at the 1932 A.A.U. Championships and the results duplicated the Big Ten: Keller winning the highs, Saling the lows.

Positions for the 1932 Olympics were established at the A.A.U. meet so both runners would be representing the United States in Los Angeles. In the high's opening heat at Los Angeles, Saling conserved his energy and coasted second to Finlay of Great Britain. In the semi-finals he turned it on, winning his heat in 14.4, a time that established a new Olympic record. The finals were set without Keller after he failed to qualify, but former record holder Percy Beard of the U.S. and Britain's Lord David Burghley, the 1928 champion, were in the field. Saling ran a 14.6, off his semi-final record time, but good enough to edge Beard for the gold medal.

When the *Track and Field Guide* of 1933 was published Saling was on the All-America team in both the high and low hurdles. The future seemed bright, but later that spring George was tragically killed in an automobile accident.

13 – Jerry Reichow

Hometown: Decorah

As a Decorah High School athlete, Reichow was one of the state's best. He was selected to the All-State team in both football and basketball. In track he qualified for the state meet in multiple events during his junior and senior seasons.

The leading passer for the Iowa Hawkeyes in 1954 and 1955, he finished seventh in the nation in total offense. Jerry played in three post-season bowls, including the East/West Shrine game where he was named the game's Most Valuable Player. He also was a member of the 1955 Iowa basketball team that finished fourth in the NCAA Tournament.

Drafted by Detroit in the fourth round, Reichow played quarterback, tight end and receiver during his four seasons with the Lions. He helped the Lions capture the NFL title in 1957. In 1960 he was traded to Philadelphia, where he was a teammate of Norm Van Brocklin on the Eagles' squad that won the league championship. The next year he was dealt to Washington who immediately sent him to Minnesota, where Van Brocklin had just been named head coach.

As a receiver he led the Vikings in receptions, receiving yardage, and receiving touchdowns during his pro-bowl 1961 season, the first in Vikings' history. The eleven touchdowns caught stood as the team's season record until surpassed in 1995.

When his playing days ended, Jerry stayed with the Vikings taking a position as the team's Director of Player Personnel in 1966. He was named the Director of Football Operations in 1975 and became Assistant General Manager of National Scouting in 1992. His role in the success of the team has been through the draft. Players selected, based on recommendations he made, have contributed to four Super Bowl appearances and numerous playoff berths.

NFL Receiving Record

8 Seasons	G	REC	YDS	TD
Career	95	172	2,579	24

14 – Aubrey Devine

Hometown: Des Moines

After graduating from Des Moines West High School in 1918, Devine briefly served with the Marines during World War I. He then enrolled at the University of Iowa. As a halfback and fullback at West, Aubrey had been selected first team All-State in both his junior and senior seasons. He also played basketball and during track season specialized in the pole vault.

As a Hawkeye, Devine started at the quarterback position for three years. During that time, Iowa won seventeen games and lost four, including an unbeaten season in 1921. Notre Dame entered the 1921 contest with Iowa unbeaten in twenty straight, but Aubrey and the Hawks ended the run with a 10-7 victory. The winning points came late in the game on a thirty-eight yard drop kick field goal by Devine.

At that time the role of the quarterback was different than in today's game. He was called on to do the greatest share of the team's running. At 5'9" and 170 pounds, Aubrey darted and dashed for the majority of his yardage, and when he ran the off-tackle play he followed the blocking of Clinton's Fred Slater. Offenses were methodical and the battle for field position was important. The regular punt and the quick kick were the chief weapons in gaining field position and Devine excelled in both. Many of his kicks pinned the opposition deep in their own territory.

The forward pass was used sparingly in a team's offensive game plan. When passes were attempted, it was often on the run. Aubrey was keenly accurate, never having a pass intercepted. He had a particularly good game against Minnesota, throwing for two touchdowns in addition to four running scores.

His career numbers pale in comparison to those of today's top players. His 1,961 rushing yards are less than some backs have gained in a year. Scoring 161 career points is also on the low side for a three-year player. College football has changed, but throughout the history of sports players are judged by how they fared against their contemporaries. Aubrey was in elite company as a three-time Big Ten first team selection and in 1921 he became the first Iowa player to be chosen as a consensus All-American.

15 – Jim Zalesky

Hometown: Cedar Rapids

The most difficult coaching assignment is to succeed a legend of the sport. Jim Zalesky was faced with that task when he became the head wrestling coach at the University of Iowa after Dan Gable's retirement. Where others might have failed, Jim succeeded. He led the Hawkeyes to three NCAA team championships and coached ten individual NCAA Champions. In years that did not produced NCAA titles, the Hawks were highly ranked and always considered a threat for the championship. Zalesky was named Big Ten Coach of the Year in both 2000 and 2004 and the National Wrestling Coaches Association Coach of the Year in 1998 and 1999. Following the 2006 season the athletic administration decided to make a change, relieving him of his duties as head coach.

Zalesky wrestled for Prairie High School of Cedar Rapids, winning back-to-back state individual titles in 1978 and 1979. Jim had one of the most notable careers in the records of Iowa Hawkeye wrestling. The team won NCAA titles each of the years he wrestled. A four time All-American, he won NCAA titles his final three years. He ended his career with an eighty-nine match winning streak, including undefeated seasons as a junior and senior. He was named Outstanding Wrestler at the 1984 NCAA Meet, and *Amateur Wrestling News* named him the Wrestler of the Decade for the 1980's.

Jim was a graduate assistant for Coach Gable in 1985 and 1986. He served for three seasons as an assistant coach at Minnesota before returning to Iowa. As assistant coach and head recruiter under Gable for seven seasons he was named National Wrestling Coaches Association Assistant Coach of the Year in 1992 and 1997.

Zalesky attempted to make the 1988 Olympic team, but finished second at the United States Nationals. For his accomplishments as a competitor and coach he has been inducted into the National Wrestling Hall of Fame, the Iowa Wrestling Hall of Fame, the University of Iowa Letterman's Club Hall of Fame, and the Iowa High School Athletic Association Wrestling Hall of Fame.

16 – Vern Den Herder

Hometown: Sioux Center

Vern Den Herder was a multi-sport participant for Sioux Center High School. He was a good football player, but gained more recognition for his play on the basketball court. As a junior he led his team to the state championship. A first team All-State selection, Den Herder received numerous basketball scholarship offers, including some form Division I schools. Instead of specializing as a basketball player, Vern chose to attend Central College because he would have an opportunity to play both football and basketball.

He was did participate in both sports at Central, performing at a high level in each. As a basketball player he set scoring and rebounding records, some that still stand. He defined himself as a football player on the defensive line for the Dutch, earning All-American honors. Vern was recognized for his collegiate achievements by his induction into the College Football Hall of Fame.

The Miami Dolphins took a chance on this player from a small college, selecting him in the ninth round of the 1971 Draft and it paid dividends for both. Vern came to a Dolphins team that was on the verge of greatness and he filled a need they had in the defensive line. The team made it to the Super Bowl in his rookie season, losing to the Dallas Cowboys. The following season the Dolphins posted the only undefeated season in the history of the NFL, including a win over the Washington Redskins in Super Bowl VII. Vern was credited with five tackles in the victory.

In his eleven-year career, Vern was a steady contributor to the defense, earning the Dolphins' Most Valuable Defensive Player Award five times. He wasn't a flashy player but he always got the job done. Only one time did he receive league recognition; in 1972 the Associated Press named him to the All-AFC team after a ten-sack season. More importantly, Vern Den Herder earned the respect of his coaches, teammates, and the opposing offensive linemen.

NFL Defensive Record

11 seasons	G	SKS
Career	166	59.5

17 – Bob Locker

Hometown: George

After graduating from George High School, Locker attended Iowa State University playing baseball for legendary coach Cap Timm. In 1960 Bob signed with the Chicago White Sox. They sent him to Lincoln where he won fifteen games and led the league in strikeouts. After two years of military service, he was in Indianapolis for the 1964 season before a call up to the Sox in 1965. During his rookie season the White Sox won a doubleheader from the Red Sox by identical scores of 3-2 and Bob got the save in both games.

In 1967 Bob led all American League pitchers with seventy-seven appearances. After five seasons in Chicago, Seattle selected Locker in the 1969 expansion draft. After spending a little more than one year with Seattle and Milwaukee, he was traded to the Oakland Athletics. A middle reliever with the A's, Locker was called upon to hold the lead until Hall of Fame closing pitcher Rollie Fingers came in to finish. Bob pitched in one game during Oakland's championship in the 1972 World Series. With Fingers entrenched as the closer, Bob finished his career in 1973 and 1975 with the Chicago Cubs. During the 1973 season he made his 500th relief appearance, the leader at the time.

Major League Pitching Record

Year	Team	W	L	G	SV	IP	H	ER	ERA
1965	CHW	5	2	51	2	91.3	71	32	3.15
1966	CHW	9	8	56	12	95.0	73	26	2.46
1967	CHW	7	5	77	20	124.7	102	29	2.09
1968	CHW	5	4	70	10	90.3	78	23	2.29
1969	CHW	2	3	17	4	22.0	26	16	6.55
1969	SEP	3	3	51	6	78.3	69	19	2.18
1970	MIL	0	1	28	3	31.7	37	12	3.41
1970	OAK	3	3	38	4	56.3	49	18	2.88
1971	OAK	7	2	47	6	72.3	68	23	2.86
1972	OAK	6	1	56	10	78.0	69	23	2.65
1973	CHC	10	6	63	18	106.3	96	30	2.54
1975	CHC	0	1	22	0	32.7	38	18	4.96
Career		57	39	576	95	879.0	776	269	2.75

18 – Mark Kacmarynski

Hometown: Mallard

I must admit my selection of Kacmarynski for this book was a bit selfish. In the 1982-83 school year, I was teaching second grade at Mallard and Mark was one of my students. "Kac" and his schoolmates spent many recesses running pass patterns as I threw passes. Those youngsters carried on the traditional success of the Ducks' high school football before consolidation with West Bend. Mark was the best player of the group earning first team All-State recognition in his junior and senior seasons. He also was an integral part of the Mallard basketball team that made it to the state tournament.

Mark attended Central College where he rewrote the record book as a running back. There are eighteen rushing categories in the record book and at the completion of his eligibility, Mark held sixteen records and was tied for one. Entering his senior season, he was a leading candidate for the Gagliardi Player of the Year Award, the NCAA Division III equivalent of the Heisman. A broken leg in the third game ended his season. Granted an additional year of eligibility, he completed his career for the Dutch with 5,855 yards rushing, currently ranking seventh on the Division III list. Mark was tabbed as a first team Division III running back in 1994 and 1996.

Signing as a free agent with the Chicago Bears in 1997, Mark was with the club through training camp and preseason before being released. In 1998 he was waived by the Indianapolis Colts after camp, then was signed by the Philadelphia Eagles. Allocated to Frankfort of NFL Europe, Mark shared the running duties until an injury ended his season as the Galaxy went on to win the World Bowl. After playing the 2000 NFL Europe season with Amsterdam, Mark's professional career came to an end.

Professional Rushing Receiving Record

Year	Team	G	ATT	YDS	TD	REC	YDS	TD
1999	Frankfurt	6	43	192	0	9	72	0
2000	Amsterdam	10	73	212	0	14	104	0
Career		16	116	404	0	23	176	0

19 – Juliana Korver

Hometown: Rockford

We have all thrown a frisbee in the back yard. Many had competitions of sort; longest throw, trick tosses, or number of shots to hit the tree. Rockford native Juliana Korver became one of the world's best at doing those things. She put her skills to use on the Professional Disc Golfers Association Tour. As a student at Rudd-Rockford-Marble Rock High School, Korver participated in sports, earning thirteen letters. She played basketball and softball during her freshman year at Grinnell College. Those experiences helped develop a competitive spirit that propelled her to the top of women's disc golf.

Transferring to UNI from Grinnell, Juliana gave up sports while completing three majors and one minor. While on a geology field trip she was introduced to the disc. A classmate had been playing professionally, and he had his discs along. After watching him throw, Korver wanted to try and immediately became hooked. Soon she played a round in the Cedar Falls league, and within a week entered a tournament. As a grad student at Iowa State she continued to develop her game and began to play tournaments. Juliana capped her amateur career by winning the Amateur World Championship in 1995.

At a crossroads in her career, Juliana decided to join the Professional Disc Golfers of America in 1996. In her inaugural event she finished in last place. It wasn't until late in the 1997 season that she regained some confidence and in 1998 put it all together, winning seventeen events and her first professional World Championship. From that time Juliana became one of the world's top female disc golfers, winning four additional championships and multiple tour events. During a three-year span she was virtually unbeatable, once winning by forty-seven strokes. A challenger to her reign surfaced in 2001 when Iowa native Des Reading of Woodward joined the tour. The two Iowans soon dominated tournaments in the women's division.

Unknown to most of the sporting world, including her home state, Juliana is regarded by the disc golf community as an icon. Today she is one of the sport's leading ambassadors. That recognition made possible tournament sponsorships and a contract with the Innova Company for her own line of discs and golfing apparel.

20 – Joe Hatten

Hometown: Bancroft

As a high school student in the 1940s, Joe Hatten played baseball for St. Johns High School of Bancroft. He was asked to play second base, which was a little unusual since he was left-handed. After one high school season he dropped out of school and became a pitcher for the town team known as the Cubs. Joe quickly became a local hero and on the days he was to pitch everyone came to the game. He later moved up to the Bancroft Lions, the better of the town's teams, comprised of the older ballplayers. In a game against Whittemore that lasted seventeen innings, "Lefty" struck out twenty-nine batters.

Signing his first professional contract in 1938, Joe spent four seasons working his way toward a roster spot with the Brooklyn Dodgers. Then in May of 1942 he joined the Navy where his job was pitching. In the service he compiled a record of ninety wins against only three losses. Leaving the Navy in 1945, Joe resumed his professional baseball career in 1946, playing in the majors with the Dodgers.

Joe was on the mound for two of baseball's most famous games. The first was the debut of Jackie Robinson, the first African-American player in the modern era. The second was in the 1947 World Series when the Dodger's Al Gionfriddo robbed Yankee great Joe DiMaggio of an extra base hit. Hatten also pitched in the 1949 Series, receiving neither a win nor loss in his lone appearance.

Not blessed with exceptional talent, Joe had to grind for his success. He was a tough competitor, once winning both games of a double-header. He pitched a complete 13-2 win in game one, and then pitched the last six innings of game two for the victory.

Major League Pitching Record

7 seasons	W	L	G	SV	IP	H	ER	BB	SO	ERA
Career	65	49	233	4	1087.0	1124	468	492	381	3.87

21 – Denis Menke

Hometown: Bancroft

Like Hatten, Menke is a product of Bancroft St. Johns High School. Unlike Hatten, Menke was coached by Vince Meyer and played all four years of school. After graduation he signed with the Milwaukee Braves organization and began minor league play in Cedar Rapids. In 1961 he was the Pacific Coast League choice as Rookie of the Year. A mid-season call from the Braves in 1962 began a thirteen-year major league career as an infielder for three teams.

As the Braves third baseman, Denis hit for a solid average and decent power, including a career high twenty home run season in 1964. He was traded to Houston after the 1967 season. In his four seasons with the Astros, he was the team's regular second baseman (1968), shortstop (1969 & 1970), and first baseman (1971). He had seasons of ninety RBI in 1969 and 1970, making the All-Star Team both years. Traded to the Cincinnati Reds in 1972, Menke played third base as the club made it to the World Series, losing to the Oakland A's in seven games. Back with the Astros for a final season in 1974, he played thirty games as a utility infielder. Denis then spent almost twenty-five years as a minor league manager and major league hitting coach.

Major League Hitting Record

Year	Team	G	AB	R	H	2B	3B	HR	RBI	BA
1962	Mil	50	146	12	28	3	1	2	16	.192
1963	Mil	146	518	58	121	16	4	11	50	.234
1964	Mil	151	505	79	143	29	5	20	65	.283
1965	Mil	71	181	16	44	13	1	4	18	.243
1966	Atl	138	454	55	114	20	4	15	60	.251
1967	Atl	129	418	37	95	14	3	7	39	.227
1968	Hou	150	542	56	135	23	6	6	56	.249
1969	Hou	154	553	72	149	25	5	10	90	.269
1970	Hou	154	562	82	171	26	6	13	92	.304
1971	Hou	146	475	57	117	26	3	14	3	.246
1972	Cin	140	447	41	104	19	2	9	50	.233
1973	Cin	139	241	38	46	10	0	3	26	.191
1974	Hou	30	29	2	3	1	0	0	1	.103
Career		1598	5071	605	1270	225	40	101	606	.250

22 – Gerald Leeman

Hometown: Osage

As a high school wrestler Leeman won three individual state championships and his 1940 Osage High School team added the team title. Wrestling at 112 pounds, he won his first national AAU freestyle title in 1940. The tournament had eight weight divisions and Osage natives claimed two titles. Still a junior in high school, Leeman and teammate, Edward Viskocil, combined for more points in that meet than the official team champion.

After wrestling his freshman season for Iowa State Teachers College (UNI), Leeman spent two years as a Navy pilot. When he returned to Cedar Falls in December of 1945, coach Dave McCuskey immediately put him back in the line-up. Gerald lost only once that season, earning the 128-pound championship at the 1946 NCAA tournament. So dominating was his performance that he was named the meet's Outstanding Wrestler.

In 1948 Leeman won another National AAU title and topped the 125.5-pound field at the Olympic Trials earning the berth on the U.S. Olympic team. At the London Games he qualified for the final match but lost to a wrestler from the powerful Turkish team. Bringing the silver medal back home, Gerald was one of three Iowans to earn a freestyle wrestling medal in London.

Leeman became a teacher and coach at Fort Dodge High School in 1948. His wrestling squads lost only one dual meet in the two years he coached. In 1950 he joined the staff at Lehigh University as an assistant coach. During the Olympic trails Gerald made such an impression on Lehigh's legendary coach Billy Sheridan that Sheridan handpicked him to be his successor. In 1953 he took over the head job, posting a dual meet record of 161-38-4 in eighteen seasons. The Engineers had four NCAA tournament top-five team finishes during his coaching tenure. Six of his wrestlers captured individual NCAA titles. In addition to his wrestling duties, Leeman also coached varsity tennis, soccer and cross-country, and freshman track.

Gerald Leeman has been enshrined in the National Wrestling Hall of Fame, the UNI Hall of Fame, and the National Collegiate Wrestling Hall of Fame.

23 – Mona Schallau

Hometown: Iowa City

Mona Schallau began playing in the Iowa City junior tennis program after convincing her mother she needed a racket. She soon became the top junior player in the area. Wishing to continue tennis in high school she encountered a roadblock, City High did not sponsor girls sports. Determined to get a chance to play, Mona attended a school board meeting requesting the school district join the Iowa Girls High School Athletic Union. The board voted in her favor and City High had a tennis team. Mona advanced to state tournament competition in her junior and senior seasons, winning singles titles each year. During the summer months she played in regional and national events, gaining a top twenty national junior ranking.

After graduation in 1967, Mona attended Rollins College in Winter Park, Florida. Like most top high school players, she selected a warm climate school for year-round play. At Rollins she made the singles semifinals of the National Intercollegiate Tournament and finished as runner-up in doubles competition. She was selected as a member of the 1970 U.S. team to the World University Games.

Debuting on the Australian circuit and then playing on the Women's Tennis Tour, Mona competed professionally for nine years. She achieved a world ranking of number eleven and a number one U.S. ranking in doubles. She won fifteen professional doubles titles and played six times at Wimbledon. She played World Team Tennis and was a member of U.S. Wightman Cup teams in 1974, 1975 and 1976.

Following retirement from professional tennis Mona became known as Anne Guerrant, her middle and married name. She soon resumed tennis, claiming United States Tennis Association national titles in 35-and-under singles, 45-and-over singles, and 55-and-over singles age groups. Anne has also played internationally on winning U.S. teams, including the Margaret Court Cup in 1995, Maria Bueno Cup in 1999, and Maureen Connolly Cup team in 2003 and 2004.

Serving as Executive Director, Anne is actively involved with Billie Jean King WTT Charities. The organization sponsors the WTT Junior Nationals and provides scholarships to young tennis players suffering from diabetes.

24 – Beth Bader

Hometown: Eldon

While Bader is known as a golfer, she also excelled as a volleyball and basketball player for North Scott High School. A knee injury in the summer prior to her senior year cost her the entire volleyball season and all but seven games of basketball. Regardless, she left as the school's basketball career leader in both scoring and rebounds. Her years of high school golf brought success individually and as a team. The team won four conference championships and twice qualified for state. Their dual meet record of 36-2 included a string of thirty-one consecutive victories. Beth was conference champion her sophomore and junior years, then finished as runner-up as a senior. In the two state individual meets she finished in fourth and sixth place.

As a member of the Iowa State University women's golf team, Bader was the medalist at the 1993 Northern Illinois Invitational and was the team's most valuable player in 1993-94. She was a runner-up at the Big Eight Championship and is the only player from ISU to earn All-Big Eight honors for two years. In 1996, Beth was named Iowa State's Female Athlete of the Year.

Beth played in the state's major amateur tournaments during her high school and college days. In 1991 she won the Iowa Junior Open and the Des Moines Open. She added the 1992 Waterloo Junior Open and in 1995 the Quad City Women's Amateur and a runner-up finish at the Iowa Women's Amateur.

In 1997 Beth became a professional golfer. From 1997 to 2000 she competed on the Futures Tour where she posted three top ten finishes and a dozen additional top twenty finishes. The goal of all women professionals is to play on the LPGA Tour. Beth qualified for the tour by tying for ninth at the 2000 Qualifying Tournament, earning exempt status for the 2001 season.

Life on the tour is difficult, a tie for thirtieth at the Williams Championship was her best rookie year finish. In 2002 Beth posted a career-best finish at the Giant Eagle LPGA Classic, where she tied for fifth. She also recorded her first career hole-in-one in the first round of the LPGA Corning Classic. Playing in her first major, the 2005 McDonald's LPGA Championship, Bader recorded a respectable finish, in a tie for twentieth place.

25 – Jerry Smith

Hometown: Oskaloosa

As a high school senior Smith was the medalist at the 1982 state golf tournament. As a freshman in 1979 he finished as the runner-up medalist, leading his Oskaloosa team to a runner-up finish. Jerry is the fourth generation in his family to be in the golf industry.

Jerry attended McLennan Junior College on a golf scholarship. At the 1984 National Junior College Nationals he was the individual champion and led the team to a championship. Smith stayed in Texas to complete his college career, playing for Baylor University. In the spring of 1986 Jerry was named to the All-Southwest Conference golf team. Playing tournaments in Iowa later that year, Smith was named the state Amateur-of-the-Year.

Jerry began his professional career with two stints on the Asian Omega Tour; 1988-1989 and 1994 to 1998. Following a season on the Nike Tour in 1999, he earned his 2000 PGA Tour card with a seventh-place finish at the National Qualifying Tournament. After three years of limited success on the PGA Tour, Jerry played on the 2003 Nationwide Tour. In 2004 he was the money leader on the Gateway Tour, claiming three victories. Back on the Nationwide in 2005, Jerry finished sixth on the money list finish earning his 2006 PGA playing card.

PGA / Nationwide / Gateway Tour Record

2000: PGA - Tournaments: 32 Cuts Made: 20 Top Tens: 1
Best Finish: 9th Earnings Rank: 118th
2001: PGA - Tournaments: 31 Cuts Made: 16 Top Tens: 3
Best Finish: T-3rd Earnings Rank: 85th
2002: PGA - Tournaments: 33 Cuts Made: 12 Top Tens: 1
Best Finish: T 5th Earnings Rank: 163rd
2003: Nationwide - Tournaments: 18 Cuts Made: 2
2004: Gateway - Tournaments: 13 Cuts Made: 12 Top Tens: 6
Best Finish: 3 wins Earnings Rank: leader
2005: Nationwide - Tournaments: 19 Cuts Made: 14 Top Tens: 7
Best Finish: 2nd Earnings Rank: 6th

26 – Tom Hilgendorf

Hometown: Camanche

In 1974 the Cleveland Indians made various attempts to boost sluggish attendance. On June 4 they held a promotion in which fans could purchase beer, in unlimited quantities, for ten cents a cup. As one would imagine things got rather wild. As the level of inebriation rose, inhibitions decreased. In the bottom of the ninth, fans poured onto the field, attacking Texas Ranger players. Indian players came out to help the Rangers, but the fans turned on them. In the mayhem Clinton native Tom Hilgendorf was struck in the head by a steel chair. Bloodied and dazed, Tom had to be escorted to the dugout as the umpires forfeited the game to the Rangers.

Tom developed baseball skills in his hometown of Clinton. He was a good pitcher that deserves to be remembered for his pitching and not for the chair incident. Signing with the St. Louis Cardinal organization out of high school, Tom spent his first professional season with Keokuk. Working his way up the ladder to the majors took ten years. Along the way he showed durability, once pitching forty-two innings in a week.

In the majors he was utilized as a reliever. In two seasons with St. Louis he made twenty-nine appearances, earning five saves and suffering four loses. A trade forced him back to the minors where he pitched in the American Association All-Star game while playing for Omaha. He resurfaced in the majors in 1972 with the Indians, serving three years as a relief pitcher on poor clubs. In 1975 he finished his career with the Philadelphia Phillies, winning a career high of seven games, all in relief.

Major League Pitching Record

Year	Team	W	L	G	SV	IP	H	R	ER	ERA
1969	STL	0	0	6	2	6.3	3	1	1	1.42
1970	STL	0	4	23	3	20.7	22	11	9	3.92
1972	CLE	3	1	19	0	47.0	51	16	14	2.68
1973	CLE	5	3	48	6	94.7	87	38	33	3.14
1974	CLE	4	3	35	3	48.3	58	26	26	4.84
1975	PHI	7	3	53	0	96.7	81	32	23	2.14
Career		19	14	184	14	313.7	302	124	106	3.04

27 – Mike Eischeid

Hometown: Fayette

Born in Orange City, Mike's family moved to Fayette where he attended high school. Eischeid was a standout as a high school athlete, excelling in football and named all-conference in basketball. Mike played his college football for his father at Upper Iowa College. He became an NAIA All-American as a safety and also handled the punting duties. As a kicker he drew attention from NFL scouts.

Not drafted, he signed as a free agent with the Minnesota Vikings in 1963 and spent two years on their taxi squad, better known today as the practice squad. Mike's next stop was in Chicago where he was placed on the Bear's taxi squad for a year. When the 1966 season opened, Mike was on the roster of the Oakland Raiders and for the next six seasons was their punter. During the 1966 season Mike also handled some of the place-kicking responsibilities, totaling seventy points. At the end of the 1971 season, Mike held many of the Raider punting records including a 42.4 yards per punt average. A trade brought him back to Minnesota in 1972, and for three years he punted for the Vikings before his retirement following the 1974 season.

Mike participated in three Super Bowls, once with the Raiders and twice with the Vikings. In those three contests he punted seventeen times for 698 yards, averaging 41.1 yards a punt.

NFL Punting Record

Year	Team	Punts	YDS	AVG	BLK
1966	Oakland	64	2703	42.2	1
1967	Oakland	76	3364	44.3	1
1968	Oakland	84	2787	43.6	0
1969	Oakland	69	2944	42.7	0
1970	Oakland	79	3121	39.5	1
1971	Oakland	11	461	41.9	0
1972	Minnesota	62	2651	42.8	1
1973	Minnesota	66	2628	39.8	0
1974	Minnesota	73	2636	36.1	1
Career		584	23,295	39.8	5

28 – A.G. Kruger

Hometown: Sheldon

Kruger represented the United States at the 2004 Olympic Games, information unknown to many around Iowa. He competed in the hammer throw, an event that does not receive much media coverage. This native of Sheldon began his track career in high school throwing the shot put and discus; he also played football, earning a scholarship to Morningside College. A second team all conference tight end for the Mustangs, A.G. was better known for his track accomplishments, becoming an All-American and NCAA Division II champion in the hammer throw. In 2001 he was named by the NCAA as the North Central Region Track and Field Athlete of the Year.

After graduation from Morningside, A.G. moved to Ashland, Ohio to train with four-time Olympian Jud Logan, who heads the Ashland Elite Club. Kruger has excelled in an event that favors experienced throwers. A football background and coaching helped him reach top-level competition sooner than most. A.G. has progressively improved on the national and international level. In 2005 he was a member of the United States team that competed in the World Championships. After winning both the Indoor and Outdoor Championships in 2006, Kruger was the top ranked American in the hammer throw.

Career Track Record

2000 - North Central Conference Indoor, first place weight throw
2001 - North Central Conference first place in hammer and discus
2001 - North Central Conference Indoor, first place weight throw
2001 - NCAA Division II champion in hammer throw
2002 - US Indoor Championships, sixth place weight throw
2003 - US Indoor Championships, first place weight throw
2004 - US Olympic Trials, second place hammer throw
2004 - Olympic Games, semifinals hammer throw
2004 - US Indoor Championships, second place weight throw
2005 - US Indoor Championships, first place weight throw
2005 - US Outdoor Championships, third place hammer throw
2006 - US Indoor Championships, first place weight throw
2006 - US Outdoor Championships, first place hammer throw

29 – Brian Hansen

Hometown: Hawarden

Most schoolboys dream of becoming a professional athlete. Brian Hansen's ticket to the National Football League came from punting the football. After graduation from West Sioux High School in Hawarden, he honed his kicking skills at Sioux Falls College. Word got around about this two-time All-American's ability and NFL scouts came for a look. When the New Orleans Saints selection came up in round four of the 1984 draft, Hansen was chosen.

The first concern for any rookie is making the team. Brian not only made the team, he led the league in punting with a 43.8 yard average and was selected to the Pro Bowl. After six seasons in New Orleans, Brian went to the Patriots for one season and then to the Cleveland Browns in 1991. After three seasons he moved on to New York with the Jets.

In the Jets 1998 training camp, he was in a battle with ex-Hawkeye Nick Gallery for the punting job. Gallery won the battle and Brian was traded to the Packers. When Gallery failed to perform to the liking of coach Bill Parcells, Brian was brought back as the Jets' punter. When he had a couple of poor games, Hansen was replaced. His NFL career came to a close the following season after two games as the Redskins' punter.

Year	Team	G	Punts	YDS	AVG
1984	New Orleans	16	69	3020	43.8
1985	New Orleans	16	89	3763	42.3
1986	New Orleans	16	81	3456	42.7
1987	New Orleans	12	52	2104	40.5
1988	New Orleans	16	72	2913	40.5
1990	New England	16	90	3752	41.7
1991	Cleveland	16	80	3397	42.5
1992	Cleveland	16	74	3083	41.7
1993	Cleveland	16	82	3632	44.3
1994	NY Jets	16	84	3534	42.1
1995	NY Jets	16	99	4090	41.3
1996	NY Jets	16	77	3293	44.5
1997	NY Jets	15	71	3068	43.2
1998	NY Jets	3	31	1233	39.7
1999	Washington	2	9	362	40.2
Career		203	1048	44,356	42.3

30 – Dave Bancroft

Hometown: Sioux City

Elected by the veterans committee in 1971 to the Baseball Hall of Fame, Sioux City native Dave Bancroft had a fifteen-year career in the major leagues. After starring for Sioux City Central High School, Bancroft signed in 1909 to play minor league ball with Duluth. In 1915 he broke in the majors with the Philadelphia Phillies as their shortstop.

For five seasons he played in Philly, appearing in one World Series. A trade to the New York Giants in 1920 brought him to a team poised for a championship run. After finishing in second place in 1920, the Giants appeared in the next three World Series, winning twice. When the 1924 season began, Dave was on the field for the Boston Braves and served as player/manager from 1925-27. Two years with the Brooklyn Dodgers and ten games with the Giants in 1930 closed his career.

Unspectacular as leadoff hitter, Bancroft earned his way to Cooperstown as a defensive player. He holds the league season record for chances as a shortstop with 984. Dave was also known for his intelligence on the field and leadership in the dugout.

Year	Team	G	AB	R	H	2B	3B	HR	RBI	BA
1915	PHI	153	563	85	143	18	2	7	30	.254
1916	PHI	142	477	53	101	10	0	3	33	.212
1917	PHI	127	478	56	116	22	5	4	43	.243
1918	PHI	125	499	69	132	19	4	0	26	.265
1919	PHI	92	335	45	91	13	7	0	25	.272
1920	NYG	108	442	79	132	29	7	0	31	.299
1920	PHI	42	171	23	51	7	2	0	51	.298
1921	NYG	153	606	121	193	26	15	6	67	.318
1922	NYG	156	651	117	209	41	5	4	60	.321
1923	NYG	107	444	80	135	33	3	1	31	.304
1924	BSN	79	319	49	89	11	1	2	21	.279
1925	BSN	128	479	75	153	29	8	2	49	.319
1926	BSN	127	453	70	141	18	6	1	44	.311
1927	BSN	111	375	44	91	13	4	1	31	.243
1928	BRO	149	515	47	127	19	5	0	51	.247
1929	BRO	104	358	35	99	11	3	1	44	.277
1930	NYG	10	17	0	1	1	0	0	0	.059
Career		1913	7182	1048	2004	320	77	32	591	.279

31 – Adam Timmerman

Hometown: Cherokee

Graduating following the fall semester in 1993, Timmerman was not sure he was going to return to South Dakota State for his final season of eligibility. He was debating whether to play football or help on his family farm located near Cherokee. With a shot at the NFL in the balance, he returned to Brookings. At 6'3" and 290 pounds, Adam was a dominating blocker and earned his third all-conference selection. National accolades followed as he received the Jim Langer Award, presented to the top lineman in NCAA Division II.

Adam's decision to return opened doors to professional football as the Green Bay Packers made him their seventh round selection in the 1995 NFL draft. Late in his rookie season, Adam was thrust into a starting position due to teammate's injuries. He performed well enough to become the starting right guard his second season and the Packers went on to become Super Bowl Champions. The Packers returned to the 1998 Super Bowl, but this time lost a close game to the Denver Broncos.

After the 1998 season Adam signed as a free agent with the St. Louis Rams. Timing could not have been better as he added experience to a good, but young, offensive line. The Rams' offense became a scoring machine, marching to the 2000 Super Bowl championship. One of the anchors on a dominating line for the Rams, Timmerman has twice been named to the All-Pro team.

Adam is one of the NFL's most community-oriented players. He and his wife, Jana, are involved in numerous community events and charities. For his dedication to others, he was nominated for the 2004 Walter Payton Man of the Year Award.

NFL Game Record

1995 GB: 13 G	**1996** GB: 16 G	**1997** GB: 16 G	**1998** GB: 16 G
1999 StL: 16 G	**2000** StL: 16 G	**2001** StL: 16 G	**2002** StL: 16 G
2003 StL: 16 G	**2004** StL: 16 G	**2005**: StL: 16 G	**Career**: 173 G

32 – John Gregory

Hometown: Webster City

A 1957 graduate of Webster City High School, John Gregory earned All-State recognition as an offensive lineman by the *Iowa Daily Press* and the *Des Moines Register*. He attended the University of Northern Iowa to play football, lettering three seasons.

Gregory began his coaching career as an assistant at Fort Dodge High School. His first head coaching opportunity came at Lake City High School in 1965. After two seasons he moved on to the collegiate ranks; three seasons as assistant at Iowa Central before two more as defensive coordinator at South Dakota State University. He then became SDSU's head coach and during his ten years at the helm the Jackrabbits became a North Central Conference powerhouse, making the NCAA Division II playoffs in 1979.

Professional football was the next challenge when John became the offensive line coach for the Winnipeg Blue Bombers of the Canadian Football League. Then in 1987 he became the head coach of the CFL's Saskatchewan Roughriders, leading them to the Grey Cup Championship in 1989 and was named CFL Coach of the Year. In mid-season of 1991 he took over the Hamilton Tiger Cats, transforming them from a perennial loser into a playoff team.

His next coaching venture took place in his home state when he was hired as coach of the Iowa Barnstormers in 1995. He wasted no time in creating a winning environment, taking the expansion club to the playoffs and earned Coach of the Year honors. In the six years the franchise was in Des Moines he guided the team to four divisional championships and two appearances in the Arena Bowl. When the team was moved to New York Gregory went along and coached through the 2003 season. In week seven of the 2004 AFL season, he took the reigns of the Carolina Cobras, but following a one-win and three-loss start, he was relieved of his duties.

A challenge in another indoor league developed in 2005 as John became the coach of the Arkansas Twisters. Playing in the af2 league, the team showed steady improvement that led five wins. The Twisters finished the 2006 season with the most wins in franchise history while becoming a conference finalist in the Arena Cup playoffs.

33 – George Pipgras

Hometown: Ida Grove

Born in Ida Grove, George played high school baseball for Schleswig High School. After graduation he enlisted in the Army and was stationed first in New York and later in England. His time in the service wasn't long, but while in New York a fellow soldier suggested he try professional baseball after his discharge. The idea grew and George sought an opportunity.

Signed by the Yankees, he began in Madison, South Dakota, in 1921. Making his major league debut in June of 1923, George pitched in only seventeen big-league games until the 1927 season. The 1927 Yankees are regarded as one of the best teams in baseball history. With Babe Ruth and Lou Gehrig leading the offensive charge, New York had six pitchers finish with double digit wins. Pipgras was the number six pitcher with a 10-3 record. In the World Series sweep of Pittsburgh, George pitched a complete game for a 6-2 victory. He also won a Series game in 1928 after leading all major league pitchers with twenty-four regular season wins.

The Yanks weren't in a Series again until 1932 against the Cubs. George was on the hill for game three. He got the win that day, but most remember that as the day the Babe "called his shot." In the fifth inning a much-razzed Ruth is said to have pointed to the right field bleachers as if to say he was going to hit one there. There is disagreement about what actually happened and Pipgras sided with him calling the home run.

While throwing a fastball during the 1933 season, a bone broke in George's elbow. Surgery revealed seven pieces of bone and his career was never the same. He pitched seven games in two meaningless seasons with Boston. His pitching days were over but not his baseball career. In 1936 he became a minor league umpire and in 1938 began a nine-year stint as an American League umpire. Pipgras is one of only a handful to have both played and umpired in the World Series.

Major League Pitching Record

11 Seasons	W	L	SV	IP	H	ER	ERA
Career	102	73	12	1488.3	1529	676	4.09

34 – Frank Gotch

Hometown: Humboldt

Professional wrestling in the early twentieth century was far different from the extravagances called sport today. The bouts were not divided into periods: the combatants wrestled until there was a fall or one gave up. Unlike the scripted events of today, the champion was determined in the ring. However there is one thing they have in common, superstars. Today we have the Hulk Hogan; then it was Frank Gotch.

Born to German immigrant parents, Gotch was raised on a farm near Humboldt. The days of his youth were comprised of school, work on the farm, or grappling with his friends. This background gave him a strong body and desire to learn more about the sport of wrestling. Long before there was high school wrestling, Frank had matches around the area. As a twenty-one year-old he bet a stranger $50 he would put the man on his back. The wager was accepted; the match would go to the winner of two of three falls. The stranger took the first in fifty-six minutes and the second in nine minutes. A dejected Gotch soon learned the stranger was the reigning American Wrestling Heavyweight Champion. Frank held his own against the champ and the spark for a professional career was lit.

In December of 1899, Big Rock, Iowa native Farmer Burns came to Fort Dodge offering $25 to anyone able to stay in the ring with him for fifteen minutes. Gotch tried and was pinned in eleven, but Burns was impressed with Frank's ability and offered his coaching services. Under Burns' tutelage Frank steadily improved, becoming the American Champion in a matter of four years.

The next order of business was an attempt at the title of Heavyweight Champion of the World held by George Hackenschmidt of Estonia. Nicknamed the "The Russian Lion," Hackenschmidt was the odds on favorite to take the match held before 40,000 fans in Chicago on April 3, 1908. After two hours of tussle without a fall, Hackenschmidt conceded the title to Gotch. For years following his retirement in 1914, the world's top professional wrestlers were compared to Gotch. His legend became the measuring stick of an era.

35 – Karlos Kirby

Hometown: Clive

Although the typical winter in Iowa has plenty of cold temperatures and a fair amount of snow, our state is not known for producing athletes that compete in the Winter Olympics. As a member of the 1992 United States bobsled team, Karlos Kirby became the first Iowan to participate in an Olympic Winter Game.

With only two bobsledding facilities in the entire United States, Kirby's introduction to the sport was similar to most Americans, watching it on television. Fascinated by what he saw as a youngster, Karlos yearned to be a member of the Olympic team. There were other sports to occupy his time during his days at Valley High School in West Des Moines. As a 200-meter runner on the track team, he ran a personal best of 21.86 seconds. He also played football, earning a scholarship from the University of New Mexico.

After a short time in New Mexico, the bobsled idea resurfaced, so Karlos gave up his football scholarship and contacted the U.S. Olympic Committee. They put him in touch with the coaches; then he was off to Lake Placid, New York, to find out if he had the ability to make the team. While some thought him foolish, he had the size, strength, and foot-speed to earn a position on the team.

In 1989, after only two years in the sport, Karlos was selected as the U.S. Olympic Committee Athlete of the Year. As a member of a four-man sled team, his job as a side-pusher was to utilize his strength and running ability to push the sled to maximum speed at the start of the run. Karlos became one of the top pushers, winning the 1991 and 1993 National Push Championship.

The team came to prominence with respectful finishes in the 1991 World Cup and the 1992 Olympic Games in Albertville, France. One of the favorites to medal in the 1994 games in Lillehammer, Norway, the U.S. sled team was in tenth position after the second of four scheduled runs. Kirby's competitive career came to a horrifying end when the team was disqualified because the sled's runners were too warm.

Karlos kept a connection to bobsledding. In 1998 he served on the U.S. delegation to the Games in Nagano, Japan, and then was a board member for the 2002 Winter Games in Salt Lake City.

36 – Glen Brand

Hometown: Clarion

For many years Clarion was one of the state's wrestling hotbeds. Brand wrestled in the community's junior program before entering high school. He participated in football and track, but wrestling was the sport where he excelled. Glen's high school coach was his cousin Dale Brand, a member of the 1936 United States Olympic team.

Glen went directly into the Marine Corps after graduation, serving four years before enrolling at Iowa State University. Under the tutelage of Hall of Fame coach Hugo Otopalik he became a three-time All-American. As a freshman Glen wrestled in the heavyweight division. Although outweighed in most matches, he finished third at the 1946 NCAA Tournament. Moving down to 175 pounds as a sophomore, he finished as national runner-up. In 1948 the weight class changed to 174 pounds. Brand also changed his NCAA finish, capping an undefeated season with a national championship.

Wrestling at a peak level, Glen continued his undefeated year at the 1948 Olympic trials. As the United States 174 pound free-style representative in the London Games, he achieved the highest level of amateur success, winning an Olympic gold medal. Winning two of his Olympic matches by fall, the gold medal match featured wrestlers with similar abilities. Brand was able to out-point Sweden's Erik Linden, becoming Iowa State's first wrestling gold medalist.

After a year away from school, Brand returned to Iowa State. He won seven matches before his career was cut short due to an injury that required surgery. Glen won fifty-four of the fifty-seven matches he wrestled for the Cyclones, including the final thirty-five.

Wrestling was to remain a part of his life. With a degree in engineering, he moved to Omaha working in the hydraulics industry. For fourteen years he was a volunteer coach at the Omaha YMCA. He was also active with the program at the University of Nebraska-Omaha. An annual UNO tournament is named in his honor.

When the International Wrestling Institute and Museum opened in Newton, one of the building's wings wing was named the Glen Brand Wrestling Hall of Fame of Iowa. It honors outstanding wrestlers and coaches with a connection to Iowa.

37 – Trev Alberts

Hometown: Cedar Falls

After an outstanding career at Cedar Falls University High School including Class 1-A first team All-State honors in 1988, Alberts decided to attend the University of Nebraska. Getting a fair amount of playing time as a freshman for the Cornhuskers, he was selected as the Big Eight Defensive Newcomer of the Year. A two-year starter, Trev's senior season was one of the finest in Husker history. He led the team to an undefeated regular season and a berth in the Orange Bowl against Florida State for the national championship. Selected as the Big Eight Defensive Player of the Year, Alberts led his team with ninety-six tackles and a school record fifteen-quarterback sacks.

Trev was named the 1993 Butkus Award winner as the collegiate player considered the top linebacker. Other accolades included All-American by all major publications, the *Football News* National Defensive Player of the Year, and the Big Eight Male Athlete of the Year. Not only was Alberts a football standout, he excelled in the classroom, earning GTE All-Academic All-American selection and the recipient of the National Foundation Hall of Fame Postgraduate Scholarship.

When draft day 1994 rolled around, Trev was the fifth overall selection, taken by the Indianapolis Colts. Suffering a dislocated right elbow during the 1994 preseason led to time on the injured list. This pushed back his NFL debut and set the tone for his abbreviated professional career. In the three NFL seasons he was with the Colts, Alberts missed a total of twenty games due to a variety of injuries including the dislocated elbow, a partially dislocated shoulder, a concussion, and a hamstring injury.

Following retirement Trev stayed involved in football as an analyst for college games on CNN/SI, ESPN, and CSTV. His thoughtful and articulate breakdown of teams' strengths and weaknesses helped the television audience better understand upcoming games.

NFL Defensive Record

3 Seasons	G	TKL	SKS	INT	TD
Career	29	77	4	1	0

38 – Jared DeVries

Hometown: Aplington

Jared is one of four Aplington-Parkersburg High School football players to play in the National Football League. DeVries was an Elite team defensive line All-State selection in 1993 and in 1992 was a Class 1A first team defensive line pick. Also named *Blue Chip Illustrated* All-American and All-Midwest, Jared was one of the nation's top high school football players. On the offensive side of the ball he played as a fullback, gaining over 4,000 rushing yards during his high school career.

Jared became an integral part of the Iowa Hawkeye defensive line. In his career he accumulated 260 tackles and finished as the school's all-time leader with forty-two sacks and seventy-eight tackles for loss. He was named first-team All-Big Ten in each of his last three seasons and a second-team All-America selection as a junior in 1997.

Selected by Detroit in the third round of the 1999 draft, he became a valuable member of the Lions defensive line and special teams. With just a handful of defensive starts, his contribution is versatility as a back-up to a couple of line positions.

During an off-season workout in 2002, Jared suffered a blood clot in his right arm that nearly cost him his life, much less his NFL career. Following surgery he was able to regain weight and strength lost due to the injury. For the effort he made to resume his career, he was the recipient of the Ed Block Courage Award presented by the East Side Athletic Club of Baltimore.

NFL Defensive Record

Year	Team	G	TKL	INT	SKS	FF	FR	TD
1999	Detroit	2	0	0	0	0	0	0
2000	Detroit	15	35	0	0	1	1	0
2001	Detroit	11	9	0	0	0	0	0
2002	Detroit	10	17	0	1	0	0	0
2003	Detroit	13	17	0	1	2	0	0
2004	Detroit	15	25	0	3	0	0	0
2005	Detroit	16	22	0	3	0	0	0
Career		82	104	0	8	3	1	0

39 – Red Faber

Hometown: Cascade

Hall of Fame pitcher Red Faber was one of the last legal spitball pitchers in the American League. Red attended St. Joseph's Academy in Dubuque before attending Sacred Heart College in Prairie du Chien, Wisconsin. In 1909 he left school to begin a career in professional baseball. He began well, pitching a perfect game in 1910, but he developed a sore arm. From that setback he learned how to throw the spitball, a pitch that saved his career.

In 1914 he broke in with the Chicago White Sox, the only major league club he played with during a twenty-season career. That first year he started nineteen games and relieved in twenty-one others. He won ten games and led the league with four saves. The pattern of starts and relief appearances would continue for the next few seasons. In 1917 he had a record of 16-13, but his best pitching came in the World Series against the New York Giants. After winning game two in Chicago, he lost game four on the road. Pitching as a reliever in game five, he picked up the win and then went the distance two days later for the series-clinching win by a 4-2 score.

Faber spent most of 1918 in the Navy due to World War I. He returned in 1919 only to develop arm trouble and suffered from a crippling illness that kept him out of the 1919 Series. That Series became well known for the scandal perpetrated by several White Sox players. Red enjoyed the greatest success of his career in the early 1920s. The spitball had been ruled illegal with Faber one of the seventeen pitchers permitted to use it for the remainder of their careers. This pitch, along with the spaciousness of Comisky Park helped Red become the league's top pitcher. From 1920 to 1922, he posted win totals of twenty-three, twenty-five, and twenty-one. He led the league in earned runs and was among the league leaders in strikeouts each year. In his final three seasons Faber again returned to relief pitching. After retiring he coached for several seasons with the White Sox.

Major League Pitching Record

20 Seasons	W	L	IP	H	ER	BB	SO	ERA
Career	254	213	4086.7	4106	1430	1213	1471	3.15

40 – Dedric Ward

Hometown: Cedar Rapids

A track and football star for Cedar Rapids Washington High School, Ward was named the 1992 Mississippi Valley Football Player of the Year and Elite Team defensive back by the *Des Moines Register*. Staying in state, he headed for UNI to play football.

As a Panther, Dedric became one of the top receivers in NCAA Division I-A history. He is the only receiver in Gateway Conference history to have three 1,000 yards receiving seasons. In both his junior and senior seasons, he was named conference Offensive Player of the Year and consensus All-America selection as a senior. He holds five school records: career passes caught (176), receiving yards in a game (247), season receiving yards (1,169), career receiving yards (3,876), and career touchdown receptions (41).

A third round selection of the New York Jets in 1997, Ward became the team's return specialist and a backup receiver. He had his best receiving season in 2000 when he caught fifty-four passes. Signing as a free agent with the Miami Dolphins in 2001, Dedric seemed ready to be one of their top receivers. The reality was that his skills did not fit into the Dolphins scheme and he was released after two mediocre seasons.

It looked like his career might end in 2003 after a September release by New England, but when the Patriots needed a receiver he was re-signed. His playing time was limited, but he did get to play on a Super Bowl champion team. An injury-plagued year in Dallas rounded out his playing days.

NFL Receiving Record

Year	Team	G	REC	YDS	AVG	TD
1997	NY Jets	11	18	212	11.8	1
1998	NY Jets	16	25	477	19.1	4
1999	NY Jets	16	22	325	14.8	3
2000	NY Jets	16	54	801	14.8	3
2001	Miami	13	21	209	10.0	0
2002	Miami	16	19	172	9.1	0
2003	New England	7	7	106	15.1	1
2004	Dallas	8	1	5	5.0	0
Career		97	167	2307	13.8	14

41 – Jack Dittmer

Hometown: Elkader

After winning twelve letters at Elkader High School, Dittmer became an outstanding baseball and football player at the University of Iowa. Attending Iowa on a football scholarship as an end, Jack lettered four times, set a school record for career touchdown catches, set a Big Ten Conference season record for yards gained in pass receiving, and was chosen Iowa's Most Valuable Player in 1949. With four additional letters in baseball and one in basketball, he is the last Hawkeye athlete to win nine varsity letters.

Dittmer signed with the Boston Braves as an amateur free agent before the start of the 1950 season. In 1952 he was called to the majors. Playing ninety-three games he hit a paltry .193. In 1953 the franchise moved to Milwaukee and Jack became a regular at second base, hitting .266 and had sixty-three runs-batted-in. It seems Braves management had doubts about his ability to duplicate those numbers, acquiring another experienced infielder. For three seasons playing time was split between the two and neither posted impressive statistics.

In February of 1957, the Detroit Tigers acquired Jack in a trade with Milwaukee. He spent a portion of the season at Detroit and then was sent to the minors. An off-season trade brought him to the Giants organization in 1958. Never making the big club, he played in their farm system in 1958 and 1959, and then retired.

In the days before huge salaries, players had to supplement their income by getting jobs during the off-season. Jack did so by working at his father's company, Dittmer Motor. When professional baseball was over Jack returned to Elkader taking over the business following his father's death. He has been a loyal Hawkeye fan, attending football games and watching most of Iowa's basketball games on television.

Major League Hitting Record

6 Seasons	G	AB	R	H	2B	3B	HR	RBI	BA
Career	395	1218	117	283	43	4	24	136	.232

42 – Kevin Kunnert

Hometown: Dubuque

Kevin Kunnert was a central participant in one of the NBA's darkest, saddest moments. In a December 1977 game in Houston, the Rocket's Kunnert and the Lakers' Kermit Washington began an elbowing, pushing spat. As Rudy Tomjanovich ran to help teammate Kunnert, Washington landed a punch to Tomjanovich's face that some have called the "hardest punch in the history of mankind." Tomjanovich suffered severe fractures of the face and skull and was hospitalized for weeks. Some of the Lakers accused Kevin of inciting the brawl by swinging an elbow at Washington's head. Kevin maintains he swung at the shoulder and most evidence points to that being the case.

As with others involved in historic moments; Kevin's NBA career is often overshadowed by that moment. While not spectacular, he did have a decent NBA career. A first round draft pick of the Chicago Bulls in 1973, he was also drafted by the San Antonio Spurs in round one of the ABA draft. Before the start of the 1973-74 season, the Bulls traded Kevin to the Buffalo Braves and after twenty-five games he was traded to the Houston Rockets. Kunnert was most productive during his four seasons in Houston, twice leading the team in rebounds and blocked shots three times.

In 1978 Kevin signed as a free agent with the Celtics and before playing a game was traded to the San Diego Clippers. As fate would have it, one of his teammates during his year in San Diego was Kermit Washington. After three seasons as a backup in Portland, Kevin retired following the 1981-82 season.

At the University of Iowa, Kevin played on teams that did not compete for the conference title, but he did gain recognition as the conference rebound leader in the 1971-72 and 1972-73 seasons. Selected as team MVP in 1972 and 1973, Kunnert achieved much despite being a lightly recruited Division I prospect from Dubuque Wahlert High School.

NBA Record

9 Seasons	G	FG	FT	RB	AST	ST	BLK	PTS
Career	555	2022	558	4031	784	252	616	4602

43 – Bill Nelson

Hometown: Eagle Grove

William J. Nelson was born in Jewell and later moved to Eagle Grove. As a high school wrestler he displayed steady improvement as his career progressed. He placed third at the state meet as a sophomore, second as a junior, and was the heavyweight champion as a senior in 1945. A year after graduation, Bill headed to Cornell College in Mt. Vernon. After a short time at Cornell, he decided to enroll in Iowa State Teachers College, now known as the University of Northern Iowa.

Under coach Dave McCuskey, the Panthers were a national power during the late 1940s. World War II efforts caused college squad numbers to be low, so Nelson was eligible to wrestle as a freshman. He made the most of the opportunity by winning the 1947 NCAA crown. An injury sidelined him in 1948; then he came back to win titles in both his junior and senior seasons. The 1950 Panther squad is one of the NCAA's most dominant teams of all time. Five members of the eight-man team advanced to the finals, winning the team title by nearly doubling the score of the runner-up.

Although Bill was unable to wrestle for the 1948 NCAA title, he did recover in time to make a bid for the Olympic team. He won the district Olympic trials, and then earned the 160.5-pound berth on the team by winning the national trial. Disappointment struck during a qualifying match in London as he sustained an injury that ended his dream of Olympic gold. In 1949 and 1950 he won National AAU Freestyle titles and was selected as the country's Outstanding Amateur Wrestler.

Coaching became his next passion: first at a high school in Colorado, next for three years at Osage High School, and then on to Michigan for seven years. In 1963 he accepted an offer to coach at the University of Arizona, a post he held for twenty years. He served a term as president of the National Wrestling Coaches Association and was host director of the 1976 NCAA Championships.

A respected figure in wrestling, Nelson has been elected to high school Halls of Fame in three states, the National Wrestling Hall of Fame, and the Glen Brand Wrestling Hall of Fame of Iowa.

44 – Al Couppee

Hometown: Council Bluffs

As an All-State quarterback, Couppee left home the day after graduation from Thomas Jefferson High School in Council Bluffs. His ambition was to play football for the University of Iowa Hawkeyes. His family did not have money for him to attend school, so he was on his own. He worked his way through school while playing football on one of the greatest Hawkeye teams. Al wrote a book in 1989 that chronicles the great season of 1939. Titled *One Magic Year: 1939 An Ironman Remembers,* this book provides an insight into the men that comprised the celebrated "Ironman" squad.

After three years as Iowa's starting quarterback, Couppee was a twentieth round selection of the Washington Redskins in 1942. During that spring he was playing baseball for the Hawks when he was drafted into the Navy. In those days there was usually a football team in training camps and Al played with the Iowa Navy Pre-Flight Seahawks. He was next stationed at Mt. Vernon to set up a Naval Flight Prepatory School; then he spent two years in the South Pacific.

In 1946 he finally played with the Redskins, as a fullback and linebacker. After the season he hung up the cleats and turned to broadcasting. He began at KRNT in Des Moines and was there until 1959. He then operated a gas station in Des Moines and made an unsuccessful attempt to be Polk County Sheriff. After a move to California in 1961, he became the original announcer of the San Diego Chargers. With his baseball background, he also broadcast Padre games and was a sports director for a radio/TV station in San Diego. The southern California area became home and Al chose to stay after retiring.

Throughout his retirement, Al continued to come back to various Hawkeye games and always spoke of the 1939 season. He relentlessly praised his coaches and teammates, especially halfback Nile Kinnick.

NFL Game Record

1946 Was: 7 Games, 3 rushes for 22 yds

45 – Jamie Williams

Hometown: Davenport

While some NFL retirees opt for the golf course and plenty of time relaxing, Williams has taken a different approach. He has delved into a variety of activities. This Davenport native received his degree from Nebraska while playing football for the Cornhuskers, then finished his masters in mass communication, and received a doctorate in organization and leadership management from the University of San Francisco. He also used his football skills as a writer and technical advisor for the movie "Any Given Sunday." He is the founder and Creative Director of *YMotion Media, Inc.*, a San Francisco-based production company that focuses on the development and production of original sports-related entertainment content for film, television, and corporate messaging.

Selected by the New York Giants in round three of the 1983 draft, Jamie saw action in one game after a trade to the St. Louis Cardinals. Acquired by Houston in 1984, he had his most productive receiving statistics during his five seasons with the Oilers. A starter in Houston, Jamie's next moved to San Francisco, which meant less playing time, but was a chance to play with a team that consistently challenged for the league title. During his five years with the Forty-Niners, Jamie played on two Super Bowl winning teams. In Super Bowl XXIV he caught one pass for seven yards.

Jamie and fellow Davenport native Roger Craig are one of the very few tandems that were teammates in high school, college and professional football. At Davenport Central High School Jamie was a *Parade* All-American as a tight end, helping the team win the 1976 state championship. An All-State and All-American basketball player, Williams also competed on the track team. Throwing the discus was his specialty, qualifying for the state finals.

NFL Receiving Record

12 Seasons	G	REC	YDS	TD
Career	160	181	1980	11

46 – Earl Whitehill

Hometown: Cedar Rapids

Born and reared in Cedar Rapids, Whitehill played baseball in the Cedar Rapids area where big league scout Cy Slapnicka, also a native of Cedar Rapids, saw him play. The Detroit Tigers signed Earl based on Slapnicka's recommendation. He was sent to Des Moines in 1919 before spending time at Columbia and Birmingham. In a two-year span he won fifty-four games for Birmingham, prompting a promotion to the big league club in Detroit.

During the next ten seasons, Earl was a starting pitcher for the Tigers. One of the better control pitchers of his era, he won 133 games while losing 120 for Detroit. After a 16-12 record in 1932, the Tigers may have thought Earl's better days were behind and made a trade with the Washington Senators. Whitehill responded by leading the league in starts, posting a 22-8 record as he helped the club to a World Series championship. After three more winning seasons in Washington, he pitched two years in Cleveland and one for the Cubs before retiring.

Major League Pitching Record

Year	Team	W	L	SV	IP	H	R	ER	ERA
1923	DET	2	0	0	33.0	22	14	10	2.73
1924	DET	17	9	0	233.0	260	125	100	3.86
1925	DET	11	11	2	239.3	267	135	124	4.66
1926	DET	16	13	0	252.3	271	136	112	3.99
1927	DET	16	14	3	236.0	238	110	88	3.36
1928	DET	11	16	0	196.3	214	131	94	4.31
1929	DET	14	15	1	245.3	267	147	126	4.62
1930	DET	17	13	1	220.7	248	139	104	4.24
1931	DET	13	16	0	271.3	287	152	123	4.08
1932	DET	16	12	0	244.0	255	136	123	4.54
1933	WSH	22	8	1	270.0	271	112	100	3.33
1934	WSH	14	11	0	235.0	269	129	118	4.52
1935	WSH	14	13	0	279.3	318	149	133	4.29
1936	WSH	14	11	0	212.3	252	124	115	4.87
1937	CLE	8	8	2	147.0	189	111	106	6.49
1938	CLE	9	8	0	160.3	187	109	99	5.56
1939	CHC	4	7	5	189.3	102	59	51	5.14
Career		218	185	11	3564.7	3917	2018	1726	4.36

47 – Buck Shaw

Hometown: Stuart

Born in Mitchellville, Buck and his family moved to Stuart when he was ten. At that time the high school in Stuart had stopped playing football due to an on-field fatality. In his senior year the sport was revived and Stuart played three games that season. Buck attended Creighton University in 1918 before transferring to Notre Dame. Shaw was a tackle on the Knute Rockne coached teams of 1919 to 1921 that only lost one game, a 10-7 setback to the Hawks of Iowa in 1921. Buck was named an All-America tackle in 1919, 1920 and 1921.

Shaw immediately went into college coaching with stops at North Carolina State and Nevada before becoming head coach at Santa Clara from 1936 to 1942. He led the Broncos to national prominence, winning the first ever Sugar Bowl game in 1936.

Shaw became the San Francisco Forty-Niner's first head coach in 1946. In nine seasons at San Francisco he compiled a record of 72-40-4. Following a stint as the original Air Force Academy head football coach, he returned to the NFL coaching ranks with the Eagles in 1958. He led the 1960 squad to a 10-2 record and an NFL Championship by defeating Green Bay in the title game.

Professional Coaching Record

Year	Team	Record
1946	SF 49ers	9-5
1947	SF 49ers	8-4-2
1948	SF 49ers	12-2
1949	SF 49ers	9-3 AAFC Runner-up
1950	SF 49ers	3-9
1951	SF 49ers	7-4-1
1952	SF 49ers	7-5
1953	SF 49ers	9-3
1954	SF 49ers	7-4-1
1958	Phil Eagles	2-9-1
1959	Phil Eagles	7-5
1960	Phil Eagles	10-2 Won NFL Championship
Career		52-43-3

48 – Natasha Kaiser

Hometown: Des Moines

As a sprinter for Roosevelt High School, Natasha Kaiser was a nine-time state track champion, winning the 1985 state 200-meter title in record time. She still holds state all-time records in the 100-meter and 400-meter events. She was a member of Roosevelt's sprint medley team that holds three records: state best time, state meet, and Drake Relays. In 1985 Natasha was the first recipient of the Gerry Cooley Award given to the outstanding high school girl's performer at the Drake Relays.

Natasha continued a track career at the University of Missouri. A six-time NCAA All-American, she set a national collegiate record of 51.92 in the 400-meters at the 1989 NCAA Indoor Championships. She won five Big Eight Conference titles and was named the 1989 Big Eight Female Athlete of the Year.

A member of sixteen national track teams, Kaiser was selected because of her versatility and her willingness to sacrifice personal good for that of the team. Topping her list of track accomplishments was winning a silver medal at the 1992 Olympic games in Barcelona as a member of the U.S. 1600-meter relay team. She was a member of two other 1600-meter teams that set records: a world record at the 1993 World Championships and an American record en route to winning the silver medal at the 1997 World Indoor Championships. Her best individual event year came in 1993, winning a 400-meter silver medal at the 1993 World Championships and gaining a number two world ranking. A foot injury in 1995 nearly ended her running career but she fought back to earn a spot on a second Olympic team in 1996.

Drake has been special to Natasha. She competed in sixteen Relays; winning high school, college, and open titles. In 1995 she was inducted into the Drake Relays Athletes Hall of Fame. After serving eight years as an assistant coach at Missouri, Natasha was hired as the women's head track coach at Drake University in 2000. In 2004 she added men's coaching responsibilities. Under her tutelage the Bulldog runners have established nine school records.

49 – Dick Hoerner

Hometown: Dubuque

Hoerner began his football career at Dubuque High as a fullback on Rams teams that won Mississippi Valley Conference championships in 1939 and 1940. Following both seasons Dick was selected All-State, second team in 1939 and first team in 1940.

After one year at the University of Iowa, Dick entered the military where he also had the opportunity to play football. Returning to the gridiron for the Hawkeyes, he played in 1946 and was named first team All-Big Ten and was named to the All-American team. With one season of collegiate eligibility remaining, he opted to become a professional. Dick had been drafted by the Cleveland Browns in 1945; instead he signed in 1947 with Los Angeles Rams.

Hoerner became a part of the Rams backfield known as the "Bull Elephant Backfield." Dick, Paul "Tank" Younger, and Deacon Dan Towler each weighed around 230 pounds and the offense was designed to overpower the opposition for gains of four or five yards. When teams would bring in additional size to stop the "bulls," the Rams would counter with backs possessing quickness and speed. This formula seemed to work as the Rams played in the 1950 and 1951 NFL championship games. In 1950 they lost by a field goal to the Browns, but avenged the loss by taking the championship in 1951 over the Browns by a touchdown.

In June of 1952 the Rams traded Hoerner and ten other players to the Dallas Texans for the draft rights of Les Richter. Dick played one season in Dallas before his retirement. During a six-year career, he was selected to a pair of All-Pro teams. Twice he led the Rams in rushing and during the championship season of 1951 was the team's touchdowns scored leader.

NFL Rushing and Receiving Record

		Rushing			Receiving		
6 Seasons	Games	ATT	YDS	TD	REC	YDS	TD
Career	63	506	2172	20	80	1180	4

50 – Hank Severeid

Hometown: Story City

Severeid was one of the most durable catchers in the history of baseball. Combining both minor and major league experience he totaled nearly 2,400 games behind the plate. Hank appeared in over 100 games every year from 1916 through 1924, except for 1918, when he was in the military service during World War I.

Life around baseball began when his older brother formed a town team in Story City. Hank started as the water boy and at fourteen became the regular catcher. His first taste of professional ball came in 1909 when he signed with the Burlington team of the Central Association. The following season he played for Omaha and at season's end was sold to Cincinnati. In 1911 he made his major league debut, the third youngest player in the league that season.

After spending three years with the Redlegs, Hank became the St. Louis Browns regular catcher following a trade. During the next eleven seasons, he was fixture in the Browns' lineup, including the 1917 season when he caught no-hitters on successive days, the only time that has happened. His final two major league seasons were with pennant winners, the 1925 Senators and the 1926 Yankees. In his twenty-six World Series plate appearances he collected seven hits, one walk, and one run-batted-in.

Unsigned by a major league team in 1927, Severeid caught eleven more years in the minor leagues. He batted over .300 for five seasons in Pacific Coast League play. Hank spent the next few years as player-manager for teams in the Texas and Western Leagues. When on-field positions weren't available, Hank stayed in baseball by serving as a scout until his death in 1968.

Major League Hitting Record

15 Seasons	G	AB	R	H	2B	3B	HR	RBI	BA
Career	1390	4312	408	1245	204	42	17	539	.289

51 – Gary Thompson

Hometown: Roland

Thompson has been in many "David versus Goliath" sporting battles. As a 5'6" sophomore guard for Roland High School, Gary led his team to the 1951 basketball state championship game. This time Goliath won as Davenport claimed the title with a 50-40 victory. In the quarterfinal and semifinal games, tiny Roland High knocked off heavily favored Waterloo West and Des Moines East. Statewide attention to this Cinderella team put Roland on the basketball map and brought celebrity status to Thompson, publicly nicknamed the "Roland Rocket." The team returned to the state tournament the next two years finishing fourth on both occasions. Gary's point production increased every year averaging twenty-five points a game as a senior with 2,042 career points, the first Iowa player to top the 2,000 mark.

An excellent baseball player, Thompson played shortstop and pitched. His dad had been the manager for the town team so Gary grew up around the diamond, helping when needed. He was an excellent hitter and one of the top pitchers as he led the Roland team to three state summer tournaments and one fall tourney. As a baseball player for Iowa State, he earned All-American honors and was a member of the Cyclone team making it to the 1957 College World Series, the only time for ISU.

As an Iowa State basketball player he had three confrontations with basketball's ultimate Goliath, Wilt Chamberlain. When the mighty Kansas team and Wilt traveled to Ames in 1957, the Cyclones were waiting with a plan. Slowing the pace and collapsing on Chamberlain, the Cyclones engineered a 41-39 victory. In each of their head to head meetings, Thompson outscored Chamberlain. Gary became Iowa State's first player to score 1,000 career points and was selected as an All-American in 1957.

Drafted by the NBA's Minneapolis Lakers, Thompson instead chose to play with the semi-pro Phillips 66ers. Three times he was named an Amateur Athletic Union All-American and selected as the Most Valuable Player in the 1962 National A.A.U. tournament. After four years as coach of the 66ers, Gary retired but stayed close to the game as one of the Midwest's most respected basketball analysts for radio and television.

52 – Cap Anson

Hometown: Marshalltown

Adrian "Cap" Anson was the first white child born in Marshall County. His parents homesteaded, building a cabin on land that is now Marshalltown. Upon completing school he decided to attend Notre Dame University. Baseball fever was beginning and after one year at Notre Dame, nineteen-year-old Anson turned pro with the 1871 Rockford Forest City's of the National Association. Signed by the Philadelphia Athletics the following year, he played through the 1875 season. In 1876 Anson was one of the first players signed to the Chicago White Stockings team in the newly formed National League.

Playing for the team later to become the Cubs, Anson helped them to the first league pennant. Becoming the player/manager in 1879, he moved from third base to first base although he was not a good fielder. In fact, he holds the dubious record of most errors by a first baseman. In his defense, at the time gloves were not used and errors were common. As a hitter Cap did not need any excuses, in twenty-four of his twenty-seven seasons of professional baseball he batted over .300. He was the first player to collect 3,000 career professional hits and finished with a .338 lifetime batting average.

As a manager he took the club to five pennants. After his firing in 1897 the club took the name "Orphans" to lament Anson's departure. Cap is recognized as an innovator in baseball strategy. He is credited with devising the hit-and-run play, encouraging base stealing, and utilizing a pitching rotation. He was the first manager to use pre-season training, the ritual now known as spring training. Sadly, Anson is also known for his refusal to play against black players in exhibition games.

In 1939 he was named to the inaugural class of baseball's Hall of Fame. His contributions helped make baseball a higher-quality sport while helping make it more popular with fans.

Professional Hitting Record

27 Seasons	G	AB	R	H	2B	3B	HR	RBI	BA
Career	2523	10,277	1996	3178	581	142	97	2076	.338

53 – Don Perkins

Hometown: Waterloo

As a first team All-State running back on the undefeated Waterloo West High School team of 1955, one would imagine the University of Iowa coaching staff attempting to recruit this local talent. The call never came and Don headed for the University of New Mexico. Before the start of his sophomore season, Coe College graduate Marv Levy took the reigns as New Mexico's head coach. The combination worked well together and during his final two collegiate seasons Perkins was one of the nation's leading collegiate rushers.

His entry into the professional ranks came about in an uncustomary way. In 1960 a Dallas-based group signed Don to a personal-services contract prior to the draft. This meant he would play for them if they were awarded a NFL franchise. The Baltimore Colts took a chance by drafting him in round nine, but when the Cowboys became a reality Don was a charter member.

After a broken foot sidelined him for the 1960 season, Perkins became a fixture in the Dallas backfield. With a team-leading 815 rushing yards, Don was selected as the 1961 NFL Rookie of the Year. He followed with 945 yards in 1962 and was named to his first of five Pro Bowl teams. In the later years of his career Don played more as a fullback, displaying extraordinary blocking skills for a player of only 200 pounds. Retiring after eight seasons, he had never totaled 1,000 yards in a season, but only four NFL backs had rushed for more yards than his total of 6,217.

Returning to Sante Fe after football, Don worked as a football analyst for CBS and other independent networks. He also became the director of the state's WIN program, a work incentive program for welfare recipients. In 1976 the Cowboys honored Don by placing him in their "Ring of Honor."

NFL Rushing and Receiving Record

		Rushing			Receiving		
8 Seasons	G	ATT	YDS	TD	REC	YDS	TD
Career	107	1500	6217	42	146	1310	3

54 – Nick Collison

Hometown: Iowa Falls

Nick Collison was born in Orange City when his father was coaching basketball at Granville Spaulding High School. Dave Collison later took a job with Iowa Falls Community School and coached Nick and his team to a three year record of 101-1 and two state championships. Nick was selected to the Class 3A first team and shared 1999 Mr. Basketball honors with Kirk Hinrich. He was a second team high school All-American and played in the McDonalds All-America game, scoring sixteen points to help the West team achieve a victory.

Nick's accomplishments as a college player and on the United States national teams are such it is best to compile a list.

2000 - All-Big Twelve Freshman Team, Conference Honorable Mention
2001 - All-Big Twelve Conference First Team
2002 - Associated Press All-America Honorable Mention
All-Big Twelve Conference First Team
2003 - Consensus All-America First Team, National Player of the Year
Big Twelve Player of the Year, All-Big Twelve First Team
NCAA All-Final Four Team
2001, 02, 03 - Academic All-Big Twelve Conference

1998 - USA Basketball Men's Junior, Gold Medal
1999 - USA Men's Junior Select National Team
2000 - USA Basketball Select Team
2001 - USA World Championship For Young Men Team, Gold Medal
2003 - USA Senior National Team
2004 - USA Olympic Team

NBA Record
2003 - 12th overall selection by the Seattle Supersonics in NBA Draft

Year	Team	G	FG	3FG	FT	RB	AST	ST	PTS	PPG
2003-04	SEA	Did not play due to a back injury								
2004-05	SEA	82	190	0	83	376	32	34	463	5.6
2005-06	SEA	66	207	0	79	368	74	21	493	7.5
Career		148	397	0	164	744	106	55	956	6.5

55 – Reggie Roby

Hometown: Waterloo

Roby gained a couple of nicknames for doing his job, "Mr. Hangtime" and "Thunderleg." His job was punting the football and he did his job very well. In a fifteen-year NFL career, Reggie was consistently at the top of yearly punting statistics, earning three Pro Bowl selections. As a collegian, Reggie was a weapon the Hawks could count on to either get them out of a hole or to pin the opponent deep in their own territory. Holder of virtually all the Hawkeye punting records, Roby was a consensus All-American in 1981, the season he led the nation with an NCAA record 49.8 yards per punt average.

On draft day 1983, Reggie was the sixth round pick of the Miami Dolphins. Beginning with the 1983 season, Roby was the Dolphins' punter for ten years, never averaging less than forty-two yards per punt and had only three blocked in 555 attempts. Prior to the 1993 season Reggie was unexpectedly released by the Dolphins, but was soon signed by the Redskins for two seasons. Then as a free agent, he spent the 1995 season with Tampa Bay before going to the Oilers in 1996. In 1998 the Oilers released him, but the Forty-Niners needed a punter and Reggie finished his career with one year in San Francisco.

Known for his extremely high leg follow-through, Reggie picked out a person in the end zone stands then tried to reach him with the kick. This strategy worked as Roby is in the top ten of the NFL's all time punters. While other boys dreamed of becoming running backs or receivers, Reggie worked on his kicking and concentrated on punting as a college sophomore. As a youngster Reggie would kick footballs and soccer balls over the family garage as a means of practice. The rewards of all the practice came in high school as he was selected to the All-State team as both a tight end and punter. Reggie also lettered for Waterloo East High School in basketball and baseball.

NFL Punting Record

15 Seasons	G	Punts	YDS	AVG	BLK	Long
Career	238	992	42,951	43.2	5	77

56 – Jim Fanning

Hometown: Moneta

When visiting my wife's hometown of Hartley, we would take our children to the park to play, and at times would go to the adjacent ball field named "Jim Fanning Field." At the time I had no idea who Jim Fanning was or what he had done to have a baseball field named in his honor. I soon learned of his baseball career and accomplishments.

Jim Fanning was born in Illinois and moved to the small Northwest Iowa town of Moneta. He played four years of baseball for Moneta High School and also played for Hartley's Legion team. Following graduation he joined the military and was stationed overseas. In 1947 he began playing in the state semi-pro league in the summers and attended Buena Vista College during the school year.

Signing a professional contract with the Chicago Cubs in 1950, Fanning began a nomadic journey in the minor leagues. After playing almost five seasons, he was called up to the Cubs in September of 1954. The next two years Jim was in the minors with just a handful of games played with the big club. In 1957 he did spend the entire season in Chicago, toiling as a backup catcher. Retiring as a player after the 1957 campaign, Jim was set to begin his managerial career.

Fanning started in the Cubs organization, serving as player-manager in Tulsa and then as manager in Dallas-Fort Worth. In the off-season he played winter ball in Venezuela. In 1961 Jim went to work for the Braves organization, first as a minor league manager and then as a scout. In 1964 he was promoted to Assistant General Manager, a position he held through the 1967 season. In 1968 he had a short tenure as the first Scouting Director of the Major League Baseball Scouting Bureau. In August of that year he was hired away to be the first General Manager for the Montreal Expos.

During the nearly twenty-five years he was with the Expos, Fanning served in a variety of administrative capacities: General Manager, Vice President, Scout, and twice as Field Manager. In 1981 he guided the Expos to their first division title. After spending time as a baseball analyst for Expo radio broadcasts, Jim was hired by the Toronto Blue Jays in 2001 as a senior vice president.

57 – Jay Berwanger

Hometown: Dubuque

Jay Berwanger was gifted in many track events, as demonstrated in his third place decathlon finish in the 1936 Kansas Relays. His athletic fame was not made in the spring on the track, rather during autumn on the gridiron. In 1935 he became the first recipient of the Heisman Trophy while playing for the University of Chicago.

As an athlete at Dubuque High School, Jay participated in track, wrestling, and football. In 1931 he was selected as a halfback on the All-State first team. After graduating he turned down scholarship offers from schools such as Iowa, Minnesota, Michigan, and Purdue. Instead, Jay accepted an offer made by the University of Chicago. The offer was for tuition only so he had to work odd jobs to meet expenses. He chose Chicago not for the football or the scholarship. Jay wanted a first rate business education and thought that Chicago gave him the best opportunity to fulfill that desire.

Football looked promising for Jay. During his first year of college football his coach was Amos Alonzo Stagg, an icon of coaching. The missing ingredient for team success was a quality player in addition to Berwanger. Playing in the Big Ten Conference, Chicago was outmanned and virtually became a one-man team. Opponents could gang up on Berwanger, yet he was still able to average over four yards per carry. At the conclusion of the 1935 season, the *Chicago Tribune* awarded Jay the Silver Football for Most Valuable Player in the Big Ten. He was named an All-American and was the inaugural recipient of the Downtown Athletic Club's award for Best Collegiate Player. The following year the award was officially named the Heisman Trophy.

In 1936 the NFL instituted the amateur draft and the first player selected was Berwanger. The Chicago Bears acquired his signing rights but would not meet Jay's salary demand. He returned to the University of Chicago to coach and began a business career. Refereeing college football and writing a column for the *Chicago Daily News* allowed him to stay close to sports. In 1954, Jay was inducted into the College Football Hall of Fame.

58 – Don Denkinger

Hometown: Waterloo

Game officials should blend into the background of the game. In the 1985 World Series native Iowan Don Denkinger was thrust front and center. In the bottom of the ninth inning of game six, the St. Louis Cardinals held a one run lead. The Kansas City Royals hitter grounded to the right side and in a close play at first, umpire Denkinger called the runner safe. Replay indicated the call was incorrect and the Royals rallied to win the game and the next night the Series. Cardinal coaches, players, and fans have unfairly blamed the loss on Don's call. Most baseball experts have a different opinion, citing a Cardinal meltdown, mistakes, and weak hitting as the reason.

Born in Cedar Falls, Don played sports for Cedar Falls High School and then went to Wartburg College where he was on the wrestling team. Disenchanted with college, Don dropped out and spent two years in the Army. While in Florida he heard about the Al Somers Umpire School, enrolled, and finished first in his class. He landed a job in the Alabama-Florida League in 1960, and for the next nine seasons worked his way up the minor league umpire ranks.

When the 1968 major league season opened, Denkinger was on one of the American League crews. Managers usually test the rookie umps and Don had his share early in his career. He soon was known as one of the better umpires in the league. In 1974 he worked in his first World Series and became a crew chief in the 1977 season. Denkinger worked three more World Series and served as crew chief in the last two. He worked six American League Championship Series and three All-Star games, calling balls and strikes in the 1987 game. When the Yankees and Red Sox needed a one game playoff to decide the 1978 American League East Championship, Don was behind the plate. He is one of seven umpires to work two perfect games and was the home plate umpire for Nolan Ryan's sixth no-hitter in 1990.

Calling his last game in 1998, Don spent a year working for Major League Baseball, helping beginning umpires. After that year he retired, splitting time between Arizona and his home in Waterloo.

59 – Bobby Knoop

Hometown: Sioux City

Born on October 18, 1938, in Sioux City, Knoop entered professional baseball before the 1956 season, signing with the Milwaukee Braves as an amateur free agent. Following eight minor league seasons, the Los Angeles Angels drafted Bobby in the 1963 Major League Rule Five draft.

Making his big league debut in the 1964 season, Bobby played in all 162 games. Possessing a strong arm and having great range, defense was his specialty, quickly earning him the nickname " Nureyev of Second Base" for his nimbleness around the base. That rookie season saw him lead the American League in assists and double plays.

His best major league season was 1966, when he hit seventeen home runs. Knoop also won the Gold Glove Award and set a league record for game putouts by a second baseman. Recognized by his peers, he was named to the 1966 American League All-Star team.

Bobby spent two seasons in Chicago following a trade to the White Sox in 1969. Kansas City purchased his contract and Bobby played for the Royals until released at the end of the 1972 season. His playing days were over. He had collected three Gold Glove Awards and four times won the Angels Owner's Trophy for "inspirational leadership, sportsmanship and professional ability. "

With a desire to stay in baseball Knoop turned to managing. In 1975 he became the manager with Quad Cities of the Midwest League, leading them to a first place finish. In 1976 he guided El Paso of the Texas League to a second place finish. Back in the major leagues in 1977, Bobby began a twenty-year career coaching with the White Sox and Angels. After a three-year absence, Knoop served as first base coach for the Toronto Blue Jays during the 2000 season.

Major League Hitting Record

15 Seasons	G	AB	R	H	2B	3B	HR	RBI	AVG
Career	1153	3622	337	856	129	29	56	331	.236

60 – Kirk Hinrich

Hometown: Sioux City

Playing for his dad at Sioux City West, Hinrich led the Wolverines to the 1999 Class 4A championship. He set school career records with 1,274 points, 456 assists and 240 steals. Kirk shared the Iowa Mr. Basketball award with Nick Collison in 1999 and was named as a guard to the All-State first team.

As a freshman at the University of Kansas, Hinrich led the team in assists and won the team's most improved award. As his college career progressed, he spent more time as a shooting guard and less at the point. Each year his scoring average increased, topping at 17.3 points his senior year. He led the Jayhawks to the Final Four in his final two seasons, losing a heartbreaking championship game as a senior. Post-season honors included first team All-Big Twelve, second team Associated Press All-American, and Wooden All-America team.

Most draft experts predicted Kirk would be a late first round selection. The Chicago Bulls defied that logic, using the seventh pick of the 2003 player draft to select Hinrich. Starting sixty-six games in his rookie season, Kirk became the inspirational floor leader of the team, averaging twelve points and seven assists. Recognized for his stellar year he was named to the NBA All-Rookie first team. Increasing his scoring average in his second year Kirk led the Bulls to a playoff berth, losing a competitive first round series to the Washington Wizards.

While the Bulls did not return to the playoffs in 2006, Kirk's gritty play and tenacious defense were noticed by the leadership of USA Basketball. Invited to participate in the trials for the U.S. World Championship team, he made the twelve man squad and was part of the bronze medal team.

NBA Record

Year	Team	G	FG	3FG	FT	RB	AST	ST	PTS	PPG
2003-04	CHI	76	318	144	135	259	517	101	915	12.0
2004-05	CHI	77	445	145	171	304	494	122	1206	15.7
2005-06	CHI	81	451	126	256	288	514	94	1284	15.9
Career		234	1214	415	562	748	1525	317	3405	14.6

61 – Morgan Taylor

Hometown: Sioux City

Frederick Morgan Taylor was born April 17, 1903, in Sioux City, Iowa. As a hurdler at Sioux City High School he twice topped the state meet. He also competed at the national interscholastic meet, winning both the high and low hurdle races and placing third in the broad jump.

First entering Dartmouth University, Taylor later withdrew and enrolled at Grinnell College in 1922. There he played football and competed in track. A versatile athlete, he once broke five Grinnell meet records in one afternoon. With a jump of 25'2" he set, and still holds, the school record in the long jump. In 1925 he won the National Collegiate 220-yard low hurdles. At the time, AAU meets were the most prominent competitions held at the national level with Morgan claiming 400-meter hurdle titles in 1924, 1925, 1926 and 1928.

The trials for the 1924 Summer Olympics were held in Boston and Taylor ran extremely well. During the course of the meet he twice lowered the 400-meter hurdle world record and had his sights on the Olympic record. Entering the Games of 1924, Taylor was the favorite to win the gold medal and he didn't disappoint. He blazed to victory in a time that lowered the existing record by 1.4 seconds. During the race he had knocked over a hurdle and because of the rules at that time, could not become the record holder. The second place finisher had been disqualified so the record was credited to the third finisher.

Qualifying for the 1928 Games, Morgan finally became the holder of the Olympic record during his semi-final heat. In the finals he finished in third place, winning a bronze medal. Qualifying for his third Olympic team in 1932, he again won a bronze medal. He was honored by his Olympic teammates for his career achievements with selection to carry the American flag during the opening ceremony. USA Track and Field bestowed their highest honor to Taylor with induction into their Hall of Fame. In 1967 the Drake Relays Committee followed with his addition to their Hall of Fame.

62 – Bob Oldis

Hometown: Iowa City

Born in Preston, Oldis grew up in Iowa City. He participated in sports for Iowa City High, excelling in baseball. Bob began a career in professional baseball when the Washington Senators signed him in 1949. His first stop was in Emporia, Virginia, and then he played on one of the all-time best minor league teams, the 1951 Charlotte Hornets.

In 1953 Bob made his major league debut. Through the 1955 season he split time between Washington and the triple-A team in Chattanooga. The next four seasons Bob played in the minors and also winter ball in Latin America. In 1960 the Pittsburgh Pirates had Bob on their roster, giving him the opportunity to play in a World Series. In the Pirates' series win over the Yankees, Bob was inserted into two games for defensive purposes. He finished his playing career with the Philadelphia Phillies in 1962 and 1963.

From 1964 to 1967 he served as a coach for the Phillies, then a year each in Minnesota and Montreal. In 1970 he began working as a scout for the Montreal Expos, a job he held until 2002, the year he won the Scout of the Year Award for his work. The following year he began scouting for the Florida Marlins.

A fixture as an Iowa high school sports official, Bob refereed football and basketball for many years. During his years of work, Oldis was selected to officiate Iowa High School Athletic Association football playoffs. He served numerous years as a floor official and bench official in the boys and girls basketball state tournaments. Bob has been inducted into the Iowa High School Officials Hall of Fame and the Iowa Athletic Coaches Association Basketball Officials Hall of Fame. In 2000 the National Federation of State High School Associations selected Bob to their Hall of Fame.

Major League Hitting Record

3 Seasons	G	AB	R	H	2B	3B	HR	RBI	BA
Career	135	236	20	56	6	0	1	22	.237

63 – Tiny Lund

Hometown: Harlan

DeWayne Lund was born in Harlan in 1929, his nickname, "Tiny", doesn't match his 6'4" frame. Interested in racing he began with motorcycles at age fifteen and soon was driving sprint cars and midgets, but gave them up because of his size. He began racing modifieds, earning a reputation in Iowa as a good driver, even as a teenager.

In 1955, after serving in the U.S. Air Force, Tiny began racing on the Grand National Circuit, better known today as NASCAR. Since most of the races were held in the Southeastern part of the country, Lund relocated to Lake Moultrie, South Carolina. He drove whenever he had the opportunity, meanwhile spending his time as a mechanic or member of someone's pit-crew. Such was the case in Tiny's most memorable NASCAR racing experience.

In February of 1963, Tiny came to Daytona Beach, Florida, expecting to work on a pit crew for the Daytona 500. During practice runs a week before the race, Marvin Panch crashed, suffering severe burns that would keep him from driving in the 500. Tiny led rescuers through flames to free Panch from his overturned car, earning the Carnegie Medal for Heroism. Since Panch was unable to race it also landed him as the driver for the Woods car. In a race delayed by weather, slow going in the beginning, and marked with many cars breaking down, Tiny hung around to the end. As other drivers pitted for fuel in the final laps, Tiny, taking a calculated risk, stayed on the track. With little fuel to spare, Lund took the checkered flag, the most important victory of his career. He was the first, and in all likelihood will be the only, winner to cover all 500 miles of Daytona Speedway on one set of tires.

During his career Tiny won races in the USAC and ACRA circuits as well as the Grand American Series. From 1968 through 1972 he started 109 Grand American races, winning forty-nine, placing second ten times, and finishing thirty-six times among the top ten. He won the Grand American Championship three times and the Grand National East Championship in 1973. Tiny also won the Most Popular Driver title four consecutive years.

On August 17, 1975, while subbing for a friend at the Talladega 500, Tiny was involved in a crash that took his life. Racing lost a gentle giant, a man with a heart as large as his stature.

64 – Jim Doran

Hometown: Beaver

With four minutes remaining in the 1953 NFL Championship game, the Cleveland Browns led the Detroit Lions by six points. Detroit had the ball, eighty yards from a winning touchdown. The Lion quarterback was the great Bobby Lane, who drove the team to the thirty-three yard line. From there he threw a touchdown to Jim Doran. Earlier in the drive, Lane connected twice with Doran on passes of twenty and eighteen yards. The Lions where champions and Jim was one of the heroes, voted as game MVP.

Doran played nine seasons with the Lions, then in the1960 NFL expansion draft was selected by the Dallas Cowboys. He was the team's leading pass receiver that inaugural season, earning the first Pro Bowl selection in Cowboy team history.

Jim began his college football career at Buena Vista College. After one year he transferred to Iowa State, playing three seasons for the Cyclones. Twice he was selected to the Big Eight Conference first team and was named an All-American in 1950. He left the ISU program as the career leader in receptions, receiving yards, and receiving touchdowns.

Raised in the small western Boone County town of Beaver, Jim did not have the opportunity to play football since there were only eleven boys in the high school, not enough to field a team.

NFL Receiving Record

Year	Team	REC	YDS	TD
1951	Detroit	10	225	2
1952	Detroit	10	147	1
1953	Detroit	6	75	0
1954	Detroit	10	203	4
1955	Detroit	38	552	2
1956	Detroit	25	448	0
1957	Detroit	33	624	5
1958	Detroit	22	495	4
1959	Detroit	14	191	1
1960	Dallas	31	543	3
1961	Dallas	13	153	2
Career		212	3667	24

65 – Dallas Clark

Hometown: Livermore

As most Iowa high school athletes, particularly those in small schools, Dallas participated in all offered sports during his days at Twin River Valley High School in Bode. He earned four letters each in football, basketball, and track and five in baseball. As a senior he was named to the second-team All-State football team as a linebacker.

Clark did not did not see action for the Hawkeyes in 1999 after making the team as a walk-on during spring practice. In 2000 he saw limited action as a linebacker and on special teams. Switching to the tight end position in 2001, his play earned Honorable Mention All-Big Ten recognition. In 2002 he ranked second on the team in receptions and yards for Iowa, earning first team All-Big Ten and consensus All-American awards. He also won the John Mackey Award as the nation's best collegiate tight end.

Foregoing his final year of eligibility, Dallas was drafted in the first round by the Indianapolis Colts. During his rookie season he played well and was growing into the offense when he suffered a season-ending broken leg during the tenth game. Fully recovered his second season, Dallas caught more touchdown passes even though his total receptions were down from the previous season.

After a winless 2005 pre-season, the Colts won their first thirteen regular season games, clinching home field throughout the playoffs. From either the tight-end or slot receiver position, Dallas was one of the many weapons on the Colt offense that finished as the American Conference scoring leader. The season of much promise came to a disappointing end with an upset playoff loss to eventual Super Bowl Champion, the Pittsburgh Steelers.

NFL Receiving Record

Year	Team	G	REC	YDS	AVG	TD
2003	Indianapolis	10	29	340	11.7	1
2004	Indianapolis	15	25	423	16.9	5
2005	Indianapolis	15	37	488	13.2	4
Career		40	91	1251	13.7	10

66 – Brian Tietjens

Hometown: Kensett

There are certain benchmarks in sports that athletes strive to achieve. In the high jump it is seven feet. Brian Tietjens was the first Iowa high school jumper to clear this height. A native of Kensett, Brian's body build was ideal for jumping, allowing him to become the greatest high jumper in Iowa prep history.

As a sophomore at North Central of Manly High School, Tietjens jumped 6'5" to set the school record. The following year Brian jumped 7'0" at the Dickinson Relays, the first for an Iowa prep. He won the state meet, setting a record with the nation's fourth best jump. At the Junior Olympics in the summer of 1980, Brian placed second earning National High School Track and Field All-American recognition. He was the winner of the Hertz #1 Award, but could not accept in order to retain his high school eligibility.

His senior track season in 1981 is one of legendary proportions. At the Dickinson Relays, he established a National High School Indoor record with a jump of 7'2". At the Drake Relays, he cleared 7'3" and placed second in the long jump. He won the high school state meet with a jump of 7'3½" and the long jump with a jump of 22'9¾". He received a second All-American selection and again received the Hertz Award, this time he was able to accept.

Highly recruited, Brain chose to jump for Iowa State. In his first meet as a Cyclone he set a Big Eight Indoor Record. By season's end he had cleared 7'6", sixth best by an American. As a junior he won the NCAA indoor championship and finished third at the outdoor meet. He qualified for the Olympic trials, but a foot injury requiring surgery kept him from competing. The foot never properly healed causing Brian to forego his final season of collegiate eligibility.

The state's most celebrated high jumper, he has the best high school (7'3½") and Iowa collegiate (7'6½") jumps. He won an NCAA title, three Big Eight championships, and earned All-America honors four times. These accomplishments earned him selection to the Drake Relays Hall of Fame, ISU Hall of Fame, and the Iowa High School Track Coaches Hall of Fame.

67 – Fred Hoiberg

Hometown: Ames

Born in Nebraska, Fred's father accepted a job at Iowa State University, moving the family to Ames. Fred played baseball, football, and basketball for the Little Cyclones. Hoiberg was considered one of the top high school basketball prospects in the country, earning back-to-back first-team All-State selections. However, there was also a time he considered accepting a scholarship to play football at Nebraska. To the relief of the Iowa State faithful, he decided to stay in Ames to play basketball with the Cyclones.

Gaining playing time in 1992, Fred became the first Cyclone basketball player to be named the Big Eight Conference Freshman of the Year. The team leader in many categories, he set a school record by making thirty-four consecutive free throws. His popularity soared to the point he received write-in votes during the Ames mayoral election, thus earning the nickname he carries to this day, "The Mayor." Hoiberg ended his Cyclone career holding top ten ranking in seven statistical categories. He was selected to the 1995 first-team All-Big Eight and given All-America honors. He was also named co-Big Eight Male Athlete of the Year and ISU Athlete of the Year. Fred also earned first-team academic All-America honors his senior season.

Fred's NBA career began when the Indiana Pacers selected him in the second round of the 1995 draft. His first few seasons were like none he had previously experienced, either sidelined due to injury or spending most of the game on the bench. After four seasons with the Pacers, Hoiberg signed with the Chicago Bulls. In Chicago Fred played much more. A part-time starter, he was called on to provide stability and leadership to some weak Bulls teams.

As a free agent in 2003, Fred found a good fit with the Minnesota Timberwolves. The Wolves needed a veteran player that would be able to make some shots, and Fred needed a team that had faith in his ability. He responded by shooting a career best field goal percentage in 2004. He provided valuable minutes as a reserve, especially during the NBA playoffs. Fred became a member of the Timberwolves front office in 2006 after heart surgery in 2005 forced his retirement as a player.

68 – Cal Eldred

Hometown: Urbana

Baseball and basketball were Cal's sports of choice in high school, making the All-State team in each. As a pitcher he struck out 743 career batters and during his senior year led Urbana High School to a runner-up finish at state. He also played in the annual All-Star series sponsored by the Iowa Baseball Coaches Association. Selected by the New York Mets in 1986, instead he chose to attend the University of Iowa. While at Iowa he led the Hawkeyes in innings pitched in 1988 and strikeouts in 1989. In 1989 he earned preseason All-America honors.

In June of 1989, the Milwaukee Brewers selected Cal in the first round of the amateur draft. Later that summer he opened his professional career at the Class A level in Beloit, Wisconsin. By the end of the 1991 season, he was called up to the majors where he proceeded to win a pair of games. Beginning the 1992 season at Denver, Eldred was called back to Milwaukee after the All-Star break. He had a fabulous season, sporting an 11-2 record including a team record, ten-game winning streak. *Baseball Digest* named him to their All-Rookie Team.

Cal became the workhorse of the Brewers staff, leading the league in innings pitched. A trade to the Chicago White Sox in 2000 re-energized his career as he blazed to a 10-2 start. However, an injury to his arm put an abrupt halt to the season and almost to his career. He pitched only six innings in 2001 and not at all in 2002. The White Sox released him and it looked as if his playing days were finished.

The St. Louis Cardinals signed Eldred to a minor league contract in 2003. It seemed a bit of a gamble, but Cal earned a roster spot with the big league club. Pitching middle relief in 2003 , he posted a 7-4 record with eight saves and the St. Louis Chapter of the Baseball Writers named him Comeback Player of the Year. In 2004 the Cardinals played in the World Series and he made two relief appearances. Cal missed fifty-six games in 2005 due to a viral infection, leading to his retirement at season's end.

Major League Pitching Record

14 Seasons	W	L	G	SV	IP	H	ER	ERA
Career	86	74	341	9	1368.0	1340	672	4.42

69 – Chad Hennings

Hometown: Elberon

Hennings chose to attend the Air Force Academy instead of staying close to home and playing football for the University of Iowa. For most people the disciplined, regimented life at a military school would be difficult, but Chad had learned how to discipline himself through experiences as an Iowa farm boy, a football player, and a state champion wrestler for Benton Community High School.

At the Academy, Chad became one of the top defensive linemen in college football. His senior season was highlighted with Freedom Bowl MVP honors, Western Athletic Conference MVP selection, an All-American selection, and he won the 1987 Outland Trophy as the best collegiate interior lineman.

Draft day 1988 brought disappointment as the Cowboys selected him in the eleventh round. This was far lower than someone of his caliber is usually drafted, but there was the issue of his military commitment. The Cowboys were taking a chance, a chance that eventually paid dividends for Chad and the organization.

Following graduation from the Academy, there was flight training to fly the A-10 fighter jet. In June of 1990, Chad was deployed to England and during Operation Desert Storm flew escort and reconnaissance missions. When the conflict was over, Chad still had time to serve and it looked like he would be serving as an assistant coach at the Air Force Academy. Then an early release saw him achieve a long time dream; he was off to Dallas to play for the Cowboys.

Four years away from football meant his first season in the NFL was one of relearning. His playing time increased throughout the season, and in Super Bowl XXVII he was on the special teams and backed up the defensive line positions. NFL life progressed with Chad becoming a starter and Super Bowl XXX showcased his talents. He recorded two quarterback sacks and was the "first hit" on the running back as the Cowboys stopped the Steelers on a crucial fourth down play.

Following a nine-year NFL career, where he registered 244 tackles and twenty-eight sacks in 119 games, Chad retired in the Dallas area and is active as a motivational speaker. In his book, *It Takes Commitment*, he stresses the importance of setting priorities, developing a work ethic, and persevering.

70 – Kurt Warner

Hometown: Cedar Rapids

This product of Cedar Rapids Regis High School was *a Des Moines Register* All-State selection and played in the Iowa Shrine Bowl. After serving as a backup quarterback until his senior year for UNI, Kurt was named the 1993 Gateway Conference Offensive Player of the Year for the Panthers.

His first experience with professional football came in 1994 when he spent a portion of the season on the practice squad of the Green Bay Packers. In 1995 Kurt became the first quarterback for the Iowa Barnstormers, leading the team to Arena Bowl appearances in 1996 and 1997. A two-time All-Arena selection, Warner threw for 4,149 yards and seventy-nine touchdowns during the 1997 season.

The NFL came calling when the St. Louis Rams signed Kurt as a free agent. Like many quarterback prospects, Kurt was allocated to the NFL Europe League, playing for the Amsterdam Admirals. He adjusted well to the play on the 100-yard field, leading the league in both passing and touchdown passes.

As the Rams' third quarterback in 1998, Kurt appeared in only one game, completing four of eleven passes. Playing as the backup appeared to be his role for the 1999 season. That changed two weeks before the opening game when Cedar Rapids born Trent Green suffered a season-ending injury. Kurt was named the starter and proceeded to astound the NFL. Not only did he lead the NFL in passing, he led the Rams to a Super Bowl victory against the Tennessee Titans. He threw for a record 414 yards and two touchdowns, including the game winner with two minutes to play. He was named Super Bowl MVP, becoming one of the select few to win both the League MVP and Super Bowl MVP in the same year. He earned a second league MVP in 2001, throwing for over 4,800 yards, thirty-six touchdowns, and leading the Rams back to the Super Bowl, losing on a late New England field goal.

Injuries in 2002 and 2003 limited him to only nine games and his departure from St. Louis. Signing as a free agent with the New York Giants, his role was to prepare Eli Manning to become the starter. After ten games Manning was ready and once again Kurt was a free agent. He signed with the Arizona Cardinals in 2005 and was the starting quarterback for ten games until an injury ended his season.

71 – Gene Baker

Hometown: Davenport

Born June 15, 1925, in Davenport, Gene Baker played basketball and ran track for Davenport High School. He did not play baseball as there where no African-Americans on the team, instead he played sandlot ball. After playing basketball and baseball during his time in the Navy, Gene took up semi-professional baseball on his return to Davenport. The Kansas City Monarchs of the Negro League took interest and he was on the field for the 1948 and 1949 seasons.

With the integration of the major leagues, the Chicago Cubs signed Baker in 1950 and had him play in the International League and also with the Des Moines team of the single A Western League. His final minor league stop came for Los Angeles of the Pacific Coast League; playing shortstop he made the league's All-Star team. In 1953 Gene and his successor at short for the Monarchs, Ernie Banks, debuted with the Cubs, breaking the color barrier in Chicago. Banks played shortstop and Baker second base as they formed the major league's first black double-play combination. Since each had played only a few games in 1953, their rookie season was 1954 and both were named to the *Sporting News* Rookie team. Baker displayed great range for a second baseman and as the league leader in putouts was named to the 1955 All-Star Team. The duo stayed together until Gene was traded to the Pirates in 1957. He missed the 1959 season due to injury, and then played sparingly in 1960. Gene played in three 1960 World Series games as the Pirates defeated the New York Yankees.

A month after his release as a player in 1961, Gene was named manager of the Class D Batavia Pirates, becoming the first African-American to manage a minor league team with a major league affiliation. The Batavia club improved under Baker's guidance, partly because he played and posted a batting average of .387.

After a year at Columbus in 1962, Gene spent the 1963 season as a coach for the Pirates. When manager Danny Murtaugh was ejected form a game, Baker became the interim manager for two games, making him the first black manager at the major league level. After a return to Batavia for one final season as a manager, Gene returned to Davenport in 1965 and worked the next twenty-three years as chief scout in the Midwest for the Pirates.

72 – Raef LaFrentz

Hometown: Monona

With the ability to dunk as a seventh grader, Raef has always been the big man on the team. Playing for MFL Mar-Mac High School of Monona, he was on the radar of college coaches. He was first team All-State his junior and senior years, the 1994 Iowa Mr. Basketball Award recipient, and selected to three All-America teams. Basketball enthusiasts in the state were hoping he would attend a state university, instead he chose Kansas University.

Could his college career match what he had accomplished in high school? He started well, earning 1995 Big Eight Freshman of the Year recognition and was named first team All-Big Eight as a sophomore. His junior and senior seasons brought identical accolades: Big Twelve Conference Player of the Year and first team All-America awards. He finished his Jayhawk career ranking second in school history in both points and rebounds. The missing item in his resume, a championship in either high school or college competition.

The third overall pick in the 1998 NBA draft, Raef was expected to be a star in the league. The starting center for the Denver Nuggets, he played in just twelve games as a rookie before a torn ACL in his left knee sidelined him the remainder of the season. Successfully returning to start eighty of his eighty-one appearances in 1999-2000, he averaged 12.4 points a game. In midseason 2001-02, LaFrentz was traded to the Dallas Mavericks. After an additional year in Dallas, Raef was on the move again, this time to Boston. In a repeat of his first two years, an early season injury limited Raef to only seventeen games in 2003-04, but he came back to start eighty games in 2004-05.

While he has not become a star in the NBA, he remains a very solid player that contributes to the team's success. He scores almost twelve points a game, grabs seven rebounds, is a good passer, has good shooting touch from the outside, and averages two blocks a game.

NBA Record

8 Seasons	G	FG	3P	FT	RB	AST	STL	BLK	PTS
Career	497	2161	476	727	3286	592	257	891	5525

73 – Mike Mercer

Hometown: Dubuque

Mercer was born in Algona where his father was coaching football at the local high school. His father, Kenneth, had been an outstanding athlete from Albia and was a running back for three seasons in the early days of the NFL. Kenneth became the coach at Dubuque College and Mike attended Senior High, excelling in football, basketball, and track and field. He was named to All-State and All-Conference teams in both football and basketball.

Specializing as a kicker in college, he was a fifteenth round selection of the newly formed Minnesota Vikings. Mike scored the first points in franchise history with a short field goal in 1961. During a ten-year professional career, Mike kicked for six different teams in two leagues. In six seasons he served as the team's punter in addition to his place-kicking duties. Mike played with the Kansas City Chiefs in the first Super Bowl, kicking an extra point and a thirty-one yard field goal.

NFL Kicking Record

Year	Team	G	PTS	FG	FGA	XPT	XPA
1961	Minnesota	14	63	9	21	36	37
1962	Minnesota	4	3	0	5	3	3
1963	Oakland	14	71	8	19	47	47
1964	Oakland	14	79	15	24	34	34
1965	Oakland	14	62	9	15	35	35
1966	Oakland	2	5	1	4	2	3
1966	Kansas City	10	93	20	26	33	35
1967	Buffalo	14	73	16	27	25	25
1968	Buffalo	3	4	0	4	4	4
1968	Green Bay	6	33	7	12	12	14
1969	Green Bay	10	38	5	17	23	23
1970	San Diego	14	70	12	19	34	35
Career		119	594	102	193	288	295

NFL Punting Record

	Punts	YDS	AVG
Career	308	12,473	40.5

74 – Martay Jenkins

Hometown: Des Moines

Jenkins played only one year of football at North High School in Des Moines; his original focus was on basketball. When convinced to give football a chance, it became evident it was a sport in which he could excel. After two seasons at North Iowa Community College, Martay transferred to the University of Nebraska-Omaha. He earned second team All-North Central Conference honors and was an honorable mention All-American by *Football Gazette*.

On draft day 1999, Dallas used the twenty-fourth pick of the sixth round to select Jenkins. The Cowboys were looking for help at wide receiver and Martay had displayed breakaway speed and good hands. During preseason games the Cowboys gave Martay a chance to show what he could do. Despite a good preseason, including a touchdown reception, Jenkins was the Cowboys final cut. Disappointing as the cut may have been, good news followed shortly as the Arizona Cardinals signed him off the waiver wire.

His four-year Cardinal career began on the practice squad, then activated for the final three games of the season. During the 2000 season Martay set an NFL record for kick return yards in a season, a result of the poor Cardinal defense. During the 2001 and 2002 seasons, he was utilized more as a receiver in addition to his kick return duties. Instead of re-signing with the Cardinals, Martay tested the free agent market, signing with Atlanta for the 2003 season. Unable to make the Falcons' roster, he sat out the 2003 season and also 2004 when he was cut after a tryout with the Denver Broncos.

After a failed attempt in 2005 to make the roster of the AFL's Arizona Rattlers, Martay signed with the Calgary Stampeders of the CFL. Playing as the third receiver, he collected twenty-five receptions for 382 yards and four touchdowns.

NFL Receiving/Return Record

4 Seasons	G	REC	YDS	TD	KR.	YDS	TD
Career	40	70	987	4	151	3865	2

75 – Zoe Ann Olson

Hometown: LaPorte City

Two Iowa communities can lay claim to Zoe Ann. She was born in Council Bluffs to Art and Norma Olson and spent her childhood in LaPorte City. With the help of her mother, a swimming teacher and former synchronized swimmer, she learned to swim before she was three. Mom also taught dance and at age six Zoe Ann entered a dance contest, winning a trip to California. During the summer she appeared in a couple of plays, tap danced with the Hollywood Starlets, and placed third in a diving contest.

Returning to Iowa with a yearning to dive, a practice facility had to be found since there was not a pool in LaPorte City. Trips were made three times a week to the YMCA in Waterloo for practice during "open pool" time. This meant waiting in line for a turn on the board. To supplement the trips to the pool, a trampoline was erected in the back yard for practicing turns and flips. Not a bad way to practice until the chilling temperatures of Iowa winter arrive. Regardless of substandard practice facilities, at age eleven Zoe Ann won the state indoor and outdoor diving titles for women.

The following year the family moved to California when Art enlisted in the service. Training facilities were better and she could train with diving coach Lyle Draves, a transplant from Iowa Falls. Olson won the Junior Amateur Athletic Union crown that year, her first national exposure. Two years later she became the U.S. three-meter springboard champion: the youngest at that time. Zoe Ann would win an additional twelve national titles during her career.

Qualifying for the 1948 Olympics in London, Zoe Ann entered with an excellent chance to win the gold medal in the three-meter springboard. Olympic nerves may have caused a slight mishap as her heels clipped the board on one of her dives. It was quite possibly the difference as she took the silver medal, Vicki Manoles Draves, a teammate and wife of her former coach, took the gold.

After winning the National title in 1949, Olson was married and soon gave birth to the couple's first child. As the 1952 Games approached, her desire to compete returned. Practicing for only a couple of weeks, she managed to make the team for Helsinki. At the Games she accomplished the improbable, winning a bronze medal.

76 – Judy Kimball

Hometown: Sioux City

In the fall of 1960, Kimball was torn between attending graduate school and becoming a professional golfer. To the surprise of many close to her, she chose golf. Signing an endorsement contract with Wilson Sporting Goods, she relinquished her amateur status. To that point she had experienced moderate success as a golfer. That summer she had finished third in the Iowa Amateur, a top four finish for the fourth straight year. Two years previously, she had been the champion. Judy also had some experience on the national level. Semi-finalist berths in both the 1959 Trans-Mississippi and the 1960 Western Amateur signaled ability. As a collegian she represented the University of Kansas in the 1960 NCAA meet.

In preparation for the professional tour, she worked with legendary golf expert Harvey Penick. Her first year on the tour produced her first victory; in the tour's sixteenth event she won at the American Women's Open in Minneapolis. In that rookie season, Kimball played twenty-three tournaments, winning $4,762 and averaging 77.38 strokes. With extremely small purses in the early days of the LPGA, the golfers supplemented their incomes by giving exhibitions. That first year Judy gave more than eighty exhibitions and appeared in numerous pro-am events. Traveling to tournaments by car, she drove over 40,000 miles.

Her most impressive win came in 1962 when she topped the field at the LPGA Championship. Playing at Stardust Country Club in Las Vegas, she fashioned a four round total 282, shaving three strokes off the tournament record. After the season the *Los Angeles Times* named her Woman Golfer of the Year. During a career that lasted through 1980 she added one more individual title, two team events, and second place finishes in nine tournaments.

Growing up in Sioux City where her dad ran a sporting goods store and was a scout for the Chicago White Sox, Judy was around sports as a youngster. East High School did not sponsor athletic teams for girls; otherwise she would have displayed her natural athletic ability. Starting golf at sixteen she worked hard, stayed focused, and in three years won the State Amateur Championship. For her accomplishments Judy was a 1993 inductee in the Iowa Golf Hall of Fame.

77 – Bill Smith

Hometown: Council Bluffs

The lone U.S. wrestler to win an Olympic gold medal at the 1952 Helsinki Games was Council Bluffs native Bill Smith. As a high school athlete at Thomas Jefferson High School he participated in football as a quarterback, in baseball as a catcher, and in wrestling. Bill had plenty of opportunity to perfect his wrestling moves when his dad put a mat in the basement of the family home. Twice he qualified for the state tournament placing second and third.

Bill was a member of the 1948 State Teachers (UNI) squad that boasted three Olympians. Talking to Gerald Leeman, Bill Koll and Bill Nelson when they returned from London, Smith knew he too wanted that experience. In 1949 he won his first 165-pound NCAA title and repeated that win in 1950. The 1950 squad had two other individual titles and the Panthers were runaway team champions. Since he competed as a freshman, Bill was ruled ineligible for his senior year and did not get a chance to win a third title.

After graduation he worked the night shift at John Deere and spent his days preparing for the Olympic trials. Making the team at 160.5 pounds, Bill was poised to make a run for the gold medal. Olympic scoring at that time was such that heading into his final match Smith thought he needed to pin his opponent to win the gold. Try as he might, he could not get the pin but did win the match. As the medal ceremony was set to begin, it was still unknown who was the champion. As the competitors mounted the medal stand, Bill learned he was champion when the gold medal was placed around his neck.

Beginning a teaching and coaching career at Rock Island, Illinois, Bill prepared to make the 1956 Olympic team. Because he was paid to coach, the Olympic Committee considered him a professional and barred him from competition. Bill turned his full attention to coaching, bringing a team championship to Rock Island. After four seasons he spent a year in Michigan, then coached at the University of Nebraska. Other coaching stops included the San Francisco Olympic Club, the Canadian Olympic team in 1968, and a California state championship at Clayton Valley High School.

78 – Joey Woody

Hometown: Iowa City

At the conclusion of the 1992 Drake Relays, Joey Woody was named the High School Outstanding Performer after winning the 400-meter hurdles and the 1,600-meter relay, and placing second in the high jump and 110-meter hurdles. During his senior season for City High School of Iowa City, he set the state record for the 400-meter hurdles, but he did not get a chance to run in the state meet as an automobile accident left him with a ruptured spleen.

Joey accepted a track scholarship to UNI where he became a four-time All-American, winning the 1997 NCAA 400-meter hurdle title. Winner of multiple conference 400-meter and 110-meter hurdle titles, he was named Missouri Valley Conference Track Athlete of the Year three times and still holds the conference 400-meter hurdle record.

Participation and winning at the Drake Relays is a goal of track athletes in Iowa, and Woody has a total of nine individual 400-meter titles. He was named the outstanding men's performer in the 1994 Drake Relays after winning the university/college 400-hurdles, the only athlete to have won the outstanding performer award in two different divisions.

Specializing in the 400-hurdles as a professional, Joey was ranked as one of the United States top runners. Three times he was a member of the United States Team for the World Championships. In 2003 he experienced his highest individual achievement placing second at the USA Outdoor Championships, then winning the silver medal at the World Outdoor Championships. His running talents were also used on national relay teams. Woody ran the lead leg on a world-record setting 3,200-meter relay and the gold medal 1,600-meter relay at the 1999 IAAF World Championships.

Woody served six years as an assistant coach for Northern Iowa's track team and also as meet director for the 2000 and 2001 International Superstars Track & Field Invitational. These meets were held in the UNI Dome and featured many of America's elite track and field athletes. Continuing to teach and train athletes, Joey became Director of Performance Coaching / Co-Owner of Velocity Sports Performance in Cedar Rapids.

79 – Bryce Paup

Hometown: Scranton

Hailing from the small town of Scranton, Paup did not receive much attention as a high school football player. Only two schools recruited him, Northwestern College and the University of Northern Iowa. Choosing UNI, Bryce blossomed into an All-Gateway Conference player. During his senior year he recorded 115 tackles, eighty-four of them solo and was named second team All-American by *Sports Network*. Paup's skills did not go unnoticed by NFL teams; the Green Bay Packers selected him in the sixth round of the 1990 draft.

After four promising seasons as a Packer linebacker, the 1994 season became a breakthrough season for Bryce, totaling seven and a half sacks and his only NFL touchdown. He earned a starting position on the NFC Pro Bowl team and became the league's most sought after defensive free agent.

With his career at a crossroads, Bryce decided to accept an offer made by the Buffalo Bills. It wasn't that Bryce wanted to leave the Packers, but he never felt the Packers were as interested in keeping him as he felt they should have been. The 1995 season opened with him at linebacker for the Bills, teaming with another great pass rusher, Bruce Smith. The Bills did not accomplish as much as expected, but Bryce had a phenomenal year, leading the league with 17.5 sacks. Following the season Paup received numerous awards including All-Pro First Team, NFL Alumni's Linebacker of the Year, American Conference MVP, and the NFL Defensive Player of the Year.

Over the next few seasons, injuries slowed him and he was unable to match the stats he had in the 1995 season. In 1998 Bryce signed with Jacksonville but his skills didn't match their defensive scheme. Instead of using his pass-rushing skills, he played as a strong-side linebacker with coverage responsibilities. After two seasons with the Jaguars, he was released and was signed by the Vikings. In the one season he was with Minnesota, injuries limited him to only five games.

NFL Defensive Record

11 Seasons	G	TKL	INT	SKS	FF	FR	TD
Career	148	545	6	66.0	15	5	1

80 – Kevin Little

Hometown: Ankeny

As an Ankeny High School sophomore, Little placed fifth in the 200-meters at the State High School Championships. In both his junior and senior seasons he was undefeated in the 200-meters, claiming a pair of state championships. He also added the 100-meter title as a senior.

Choosing to stay close to home for his college education, Kevin attended Drake University. His career at Drake is one of the best of any NCAA sprinter. He was a four time Conference Indoor Champion in the 200-meters, four time Conference Outdoor Champion in the 200-meters, third and fourth place finisher at the NCAA Indoor Championships, and second and fifth place finisher at the NCAA Outdoor Championships. He still holds the Missouri Valley Championship 200-meter meet record and the all-time Valley Indoor 200-meter record. He was selected as Iowa's AAU Amateur Athlete of the Year in 1989 after becoming the first Drake University athlete to win two events at the Drake Relays.

The highlight of his post-collegiate career came in 1997 as he won the IAAF World Indoor 200-meter title in Paris. His winning time of 20.40 matched the American record.

Career Track Highlights

1988 - 6th at USA Outdoors
1989 - 2nd at NCAA Outdoors, 3rd at USA Outdoors
1990 - 5th at NCAA Outdoors, 2nd at Olympic Festival
1991 - Silver medal at Pan Am Games
1992 - 6th in semis at Olympic Trials
1993 - Bronze medal at World Indoors
1995 - 2nd at USA Outdoors, 3rd at Olympic Festival
1996 - Finished 8th at Olympic Trials
1997 - Gold medal at World Indoors, 2nd at USA Outdoors
1998 - 7th at USA Outdoors
1999 - 2nd at USA Indoors, bronze medal at World Indoors
2000 - 5th in semifinal at Olympic Trials
2001 - 2nd at USA Indoors, 3rd at USA Outdoors

81 – Casey Blake

Hometown: Indianola

Casey excelled in each of the sports he participated at Indianola High School. He qualified for the Drake Relays as a 400-meter hurdler, finishing third. An All-State quarterback, he led the team to the playoffs during his senior season. As a basketball player, he averaged over twenty points per game in both his junior and senior seasons, earning first team All-State honors and helping the team to a second place finish at the state tournament. But his best sport was baseball. His batting average was over .500, set the team record for career home runs, and was selected first team All-State as an infielder.

After graduation Casey had to decide whether to attend Wichita State University on a baseball scholarship or begin a professional career with the Philadelphia Phillies. He chose college, becoming a three-year All-Conference third baseman for the Shockers. As a senior he was named the Conference Player of the Year and earned All-American honors. Signing in 1996 with the Toronto Blue Jay organization, Casey began his professional career.

Late in his third minor league season, Casey got his first taste of the big leagues with a call up to the Blue Jays. Acquired by the Twins prior to the 2000 season, he played a handful of games for them during the next three seasons and also six games with the Baltimore Orioles late in 2001. His big break came in 2003 after he signed as a free agent with the Cleveland Indians. He was the opening day third baseman and played well enough to keep the job for two years. In 2005 the Indians signed a free agent to play third base and the club asked Casey to make a position switch to right field. Without hesitation or complaining, he made the move and steadily improved his defense throughout the season. His twenty-three home runs helped the Indians contend for a divisional title and a playoff berth.

Major League Hitting Record

9 Seasons	G	AB	R	H	2B	3B	HR	RBI	BA
Career	609	2180	320	567	129	5	89	288	.260

82 – Bobby Hansen

Hometown: Des Moines

Like most boys who dream of hoops glory, Bobby Hansen spent many childhood hours shooting baskets in the family driveway. The practice was beneficial throughout each basketball level in which he participated. As a four year starter for West Des Moines Dowling High School, he led the Maroons to the 1979 state championship, earning first team All-State honors along the way.

Hansen played in four NCAA tournaments for the Hawkeyes and as a freshman helped them reach the Final Four. Had Ronnie Lester not hurt a knee, the team possibly might have won the championship. Team MVP as a senior in 1983, he finished with 1,145 career points.

A round three selection by Utah in the 1983 NBA draft, Bobby spent seven seasons with the Jazz. After a couple of years as a reserve, Bobby became a starter, usually drawing a defensive assignment on the opponent's top scoring guard. When the team decided to make personnel changes, Hansen was traded to the Kings. After a year in Sacramento, he was traded to the Chicago Bulls for the 1992-93 season.

It was during the Bulls run toward the 1993 championship that Hansen experienced his greatest professional accomplishment. The Bulls held a three games to two lead over the Portland Trailblazers. They were trailing in game six by fifteen points as the fourth quarter opened. Coach Phil Jackson sent Bobby in as a substitute for Michael Jordan. In the span of forty seconds, Hansen hit a three pointer, made a steal that led to another basket and the tide was turned. Jordan returned a few minutes later, and the Bulls completed the comeback to claim the game and the championship. Though the first unit finished the game, Bobby and the second unit were as much responsible for the team's success.

Retiring after that season, Bobby began working as a radio analyst for Hawkeye games and spent time as the director of basketball schools for the Bulls.

NBA Record

9 Seasons	G	FG	3P	FT	REB	AST	STL	BLK	PTS
Career	575	1642	165	511	1282	947	359	50	3952

83 – Billy Cundiff

Hometown: Harlan

Billy was a multi-sport star at Harlan High School, twice leading the football team to state championships, helping the basketball team to the state tourney, and placing second at the state track meet in the high jump. He was named the 1997-98 *Omaha World Herald* and *Council Bluffs Nonpareil* Southwest Iowa Prep Athlete of the Year.

He chose to attend Drake University because of its educational program and because he could play both basketball and football. After trying to play both sports, Cundiff focused on football, earning *Football Gazette's* NCAA I-AA Mid-Major Player of the Year award as a junior. As a senior he earned Division I-AA All-America honors and was named co-recipient of the Jerry Howlett Award, presented annually to Drake's outstanding student-athlete. He became the first player to be named first-team All-Pioneer League four consecutive seasons and also earned three consecutive All-Academic honors from the Pioneer League.

In the spring of 2002, Billy signed as a free agent with the Dallas Cowboys to compete for the kicking job with the incumbent kicker. Adding to the kicking pressure were the cameras of the Home Box Office Network. Cundiff was one of the featured players on the network's show, "Hard Knocks." When the final cut-down was made, Billy, to the surprise of many, was the Cowboy's kicker.

Following an average rookie season, Billy made a name for himself in the Cowboy's second game of the season. In a Monday Night game against the Giants, he kicked an NFL record-tying seven field goals, including the game winner in overtime.

As the 2005 preseason unfolded, a right hip injury caused him to miss a portion of the season. After twelve weeks of rehabilitation, he was re-signed and in the first game back kicked a team record fifty-six yard field goal.

NFL Kicking Record

4 Seasons	G	XP	FG	PTS
Career	53	100/101	60/82	280

84 – Mike Boddicker

Hometown: Norway

The third Norway native to play in the major leagues, Boddicker was a pitcher/infielder for the high school and Legion teams, winning two state championships and making three trips to the American Legion World Series. Although drafted as an infielder by the Montreal Expos in 1975, Mike chose to attend the University of Iowa as a pitcher. He earned first-team All-Big Ten Conference honors and was selected by the Baltimore Orioles in the sixth round of the 1978 draft.

Originally a power pitcher, tendonitis caused a change in his pitching style to one of more finesse with outstanding control. After five seasons in the minors, Mike became a part of the Orioles rotation in 1983. Posting a 16-8 record, he was named *Sporting News* Rookie of the Year and earned a starting assignment in the American League Championship Series against the White Sox. He struck out an ALCS record fourteen batters, shutting down Chicago, 4-0. He became the first pitcher to be named Championship Series Most Valuable Player. Mike won game two of the World Series to even the series, and the Orioles won the championship in five games.

Boddicker followed his magical rookie year with an even better performance. He was the only American League pitcher to win twenty games in 1984 and led the league with a 2.79 ERA. Although he was selected to the All-Star team, surprisingly he was passed over for the league's Cy Young Award.

In July of 1988, Mike was traded to Boston, and in two and a half seasons won thirty-nine games for the Red Sox. He also won his only Gold Glove Award and pitched in two American League Divisional playoff series. Mike spent the 1991 and 1992 seasons in Kansas City, the first season as a starter and then as a long reliever. He finished his career pitching in ten games with Milwaukee in 1993.

Major League Pitching Record

14 Seasons	W	L	G	SV	IP	H	ER	ERA
Career	134	116	342	3	2123.7	2082	897	3.80

85 – Dan Gable

Hometown: Waterloo

It all started in Waterloo. As a youngster Dan was looking for a sport in which he could excel. Too small for basketball, he chose to pursue wrestling. Experiencing immediate success as a junior high wrestler, Dan became confident in his ability until a devastating defeat shook him to the core. After that loss he vowed not to lose a high school match. In his sixty-four matches for Waterloo West High School, he sustained nary a loss, winning state titles at 95, 103 and 112 pounds.

The winning streak continued at Iowa State. NCAA rules at the time did not permit freshmen to participate at the varsity level; thus as a sophomore Dan began his quest to be the first undefeated collegiate wrestler. He entered his final match as a senior with the streak intact; Gable had not lost as a Cyclone. The hype for that match and the attention paid to Dan were almost overwhelming. Whether this played a role in the match's outcome is debatable. Larry Owens of the University of Washington upset Gable and the wrestling world was stunned.

As he had done seven years earlier Dan handled the loss by setting a new goal. This time he set his sights on Olympic gold. He trained so intently that if he awoke during the night he would do push-ups and sit-ups until he went back to sleep. He wasn't leaving any chance that the Russians were training harder. At the Munich Games of 1972, Dan was so dominant that he won the six matches on his way to the gold medal without yielding a single point.

During the time leading to the Olympics, Dan served as a graduate assistant coach at Iowa State, a precursor to the next challenge in his wrestling career. After returning from Munich, Dan was hired as an assistant coach at the University of Iowa. After four seasons in that position, he was named the Hawkeyes' head coach. His record as a head coach is unequalled; in twenty-one seasons his teams captured twenty-one Big Ten team titles and won fifteen NCAA team championships.

Three times he served as the Olympic head coach. The 1984 team, featuring four Hawkeyes, won seven gold medals. He was an assistant freestyle coach at the 1976 and 1988 Olympics. Gable served as head coach of the World Team six times, and of the World Cup team ten times, winning three team gold medals.

86 – Marv Cook

Hometown: West Branch

During the 1987 season, Cook was on the receiving end of one of the biggest plays in Hawkeye football history. With little time remaining and Iowa facing a fourth and twenty-seven, Marv caught a twenty-eight yard touchdown pass from Chuck Hartleib as Iowa beat Ohio State 29-27. He finished the season with 803 yards on forty-nine receptions, placing him second on the team and earning first team All-Big Ten honors. The 1988 season was another great season for Cook as he led the Big Ten with sixty-three receptions for 767 yards and received another first team selection. On the national level, Marv was a consensus All-American and played in the Hula and Japan Bowls.

Drafted in the third round by the New England Patriots, Marv spent the 1989 season as a backup and was named to *Pro Football Weekly's* All-Rookie team as a special teams performer. In 1990 he moved into the starting position, catching a total of fifty-one passes including a career-high five touchdowns. Marv had a huge year in 1991, he was the leading NFL tight end with eighty-two receptions, a team record for tight ends. In 1992 Marv became the first tight end in Patriots' history to have three consecutive seasons of fifty or more receptions. Following both the 1991 and 1992 seasons, he was selected as the starting tight end for the AFC in the annual Pro Bowl game.

His playing time and catches declined with the Patriots in 1993, then as a free agent he signed with the Chicago Bears for 1994. After one year in Chicago, Marv moved to St. Louis for a final season.

Playing for West Branch High School, Marv was the passer not the receiver; he shares the West Branch game completion record. As a junior he was named to the All-State second team as a quarterback. A two-way player, he was selected as a 1983 first team All-State defensive end and place kicker.

NFL Receiving Record

7 Seasons	G	REC	YDS	TD
Career	112	257	2190	13

87 – Jay Hilgenberg

Hometown: Iowa City

It became a tradition that a member of the Hilgenberg family played football for the University of Iowa. Jay's father, Jerry, played for the Hawks and was a fourth round selection of the Cleveland Browns in 1954. Two brothers also played center at Iowa, Jim from 1974-77 and Joel from 1981-83. Uncle Wally was a defensive player in 1961-63, who then spent eleven years in the NFL. Cousin Eric was an Academic All-Big Ten defensive lineman for the Hawks in 1994-95.

At the conclusion of the 1981 NFL draft, Jay Hilgenberg had not been selected. This was rather surprising since he had been All-Big Ten his last two seasons at Iowa and played in the Blue-Gray, Hula, and Japan Bowls. The Chicago Bears signed him as a free agent and for the first two years of his professional career very little playing time came his way. Midway through the 1983 season, Jay's chance arrived and for the next 106 games he was the Bear's starting center. During that time Jay earned six consecutive Pro Bowl selections, two All-Pro selections, and recognition as one of the league's best centers. Using quickness and instincts, he was able to block linebackers as well as down linemen, helping the Bears to a Super Bowl Championship in 1986.

After eleven seasons with the Bears, Jay was traded to the Cleveland Browns just prior to the 1992 season. He started all sixteen games that season, helping solidify an offensive line that surrendered eleven sacks in the opener and only twenty-three the remainder of the year. That was Jay's only season in Cleveland, as the 1993 season found him backing up brother Joel in New Orleans. Joel was injured and the Saints needed someone to fill in immediately. Since Jay had been released by the Browns, he was available. After the season was completed, Jay retired to Chicago as a real-estate developer and builder of a golf course.

NFL Game Record

1981 ChiB: 16 G **1982** ChiB: 9 G **1983** ChiB: 16 G **1984** ChiB:16 G
1985 ChiB: 16 G **1986** ChiB: 16 G **1987** ChiB: 12 G **1988** ChiB: 16 G
1989 ChiB: 16 G **1990** ChiB: 14 G **1991** ChiB: 16 G **1992** Cle: 16 G
1993 NO: 9 G **Career:** 188 G

88 – Joel Hilgenberg

Hometown: Iowa City

It seems like Joel followed Jay throughout his football career, first at City High and then at the University of Iowa. Three years younger, Joel did not have the opportunity to play alongside Jay, rather taking over the position Jay vacated with graduation. Jay had gone through the same situation, as brother Jim had been the starting center for Iowa the three years previous to his reign. From where did the knack for snapping footballs come? Jerry Hilgenberg, their father, was Iowa's center from 1951 to 1953. It was often joked that they were the only family to play catch with their backs to each other.

Success came as Joel was selected All-Big Ten for two years and named second team All-America his senior season. After playing in the Senior and Hula Bowls, Joel was selected by the New Orleans Saints in round four of the 1984 NFL draft.

Used as a long snapper on punts and placekicks, Joel played as a reserve his first five years in New Orleans. A lifelong center, he showed his versatility by playing guard for ten games in the 1988 season. In 1989 he became the starting center, helping the Saints to a divisional title and three playoff appearances in four years. Small for a NFL lineman, Joel used his quickness and great technique to become one of the best centers in the league. In 1992 he earned his first Pro Bowl berth, and ironically it was the first time in eight years that Jay did not.

An injury in training camp caused Joel to miss the opening of the 1993 season. The Saints needed someone to fill the void before Joel could return and player personnel thought Jay was the best person for the job. The injury was such that Joel was never able to fully recover however. He was unable to play to his previous level, becoming a backup, and retiring after the 1993 season. In 2005 Joel was elected to the Saints Hall of Fame.

NFL Game Record

1984 NO: 10 G	**1985** NO: 15 G	**1986** NO: 16 G	**1987** NO: 12 G
1988 NO: 16 G	**1989** NO: 16 G	**1990** NO: 16 G	**1991** NO: 16 G
1992 NO: 16 G	**1993** NO: 9 G	**Career**: 142 G	

89 – Tavian Banks

Hometown: Bettendorf

A versatile athlete, Tavian earned All-American honors in two high school sports, football and soccer. Three times he was selected as the state's high school soccer player of the year. As a running back for two-time state champion Bettendorf High School, Tavian racked up 4,292 yards and tallied seventy-four touchdowns. During his senior season he scored a state record forty-two touchdowns and set state championship game records of 250 rushing yards with four touchdowns.

Following a red-shirt season, Tavian saw limited time as a running back for the Hawks until his senior season. The 1997 campaign was all Tavian's and he went into the season as the number one running back. He made the most of the opportunity, opening the season with an NCAA record 1,000 yards in his first 125 carries. Included in that stretch was a school game-record, 314 yard performance against Tulsa. At season's end, Tavian was Iowa's season rushing yardage leader with 1,691. He was named Big Ten Offensive Player of the Year and earned second team All-American honors.

Drafted in the third round by the Jacksonville Jaguars, Tavian had a decent preseason camp and made the team. His role was much the same as his early college career; he was used on third downs, special teams and spot starts. During his first chance as a starter, he injured an ankle and had to miss a number of games. An injury in his second season limited him to only eight games. This injury was severe enough that he was unable to pass the physical necessary to play for the Jags, so they released him prior to the 2000 season.

Tavian attempted an NFL comeback in 2003 and 2004 with the New Orleans Saints. Playing sparingly in a couple of preseason games, he was cut prior to the start of the both seasons.

NFL Rushing/ Receiving Record

		Rushing				Receiving			
2 Seasons	G	ATT	YDS	AVG	TD	REC	YDS	AVG	TD
Career	14	49	225	4.6	1	18	187	10.4	0

90 – Kenny Ploen

Hometown: Clinton

When you look through the Iowa record books, the name Kenny Ploen won't be there. Those records don't show the leadership and courage that made Ploen one of the greatest of all Hawkeyes. Kenny was a one year starting quarterback for the Hawks in 1956. After two years behind fellow Iowan Jerry Reichow, Kenny stepped into an offense created by the Iowa staff to utilize his talents. With a united effort from other talented players, the team won the Big Ten title and the Hawkeyes first trip to the Rose Bowl. In the bowl game Ploen had a direct hand in two of the team's touchdowns. He opened the scoring with a forty-nine yard touchdown run and later connected with Jim Gibbons for a sixteen-yard touchdown pass. For his part in the Hawkeye victory, Kenny was voted as the Player of the Game.

Many other individual honors came his way. He was selected to the Big Ten first team and named the Conference's Most Valuable Player. His teammates and coaches selected him as the team MVP, he finished ninth in the voting for the Heisman Trophy, and three football organizations named him to their All-American team.

Drafted by the NFL's Cleveland Browns, his skills were more suited for the wide-open CFL game. Signing with the Winnipeg Blue Bombers, Kenny quarterbacked the club to six different Grey Cup games from 1957 to 1965, winning four championships. Named the MVP of the first Grey Cup game to go into overtime, Kenny scored the winning touchdown on a nineteen-yard scramble in the 1961 contest.

Ploen had a great supporting cast with the Bombers, but he was their leader. In 1975 the Canadian Football League inducted him into its Hall of Fame. The Winnepeg organization does not retire jersey numbers, but no Bomber has worn Ploen's number eleven since he retired in 1967. It is likely no one ever will, so it looks as if it is unofficially retired. After retiring, Kenny stayed close to the CFL, spending twelve years as an analyst for a Canadian radio station.

Born in Lost Nation, Kenny graduated from Clinton High School. His prep career was highlighted with selection to the first team All-State as a quarterback in 1952 and first team All-State as a guard in basketball.

91 – Murray Wier

Hometown: Muscatine

Born in the small eastern Iowa town of Grand View, Murray Wier attended high school in Muscatine. Playing guard for the Muskie basketball team, he was selected first team All-State in 1944.

It is doubtful that many current Hawkeye fans across the state are aware of the talent and accomplishments of Wier. In 1948 the 5'8" Wier took on the Big Ten Conference with a fervor seldom displayed. In the days of set plays and set shots, his style of play was unconventional. He was more likely to heave an off-balance attempt on the dead run. Many of his opponents considered him unguardable. To some degree he was, becoming the first Big Ten player to lead the nation in scoring. His point totals set Iowa and conference records, as did the number of field goals scored. His twenty-one points per game helped the Hawks to a second place finish in the Big Ten. Wier garnered consensus All-American and Big Ten MVP awards, the first by an Iowa player.

With his college career finished, Murray tried his hand at the professional game. It was the early days of the NBA when he joined the Tri-Cities Blackhawks. Playing in the 6,000-seat Wharton Fieldhouse in Moline, Illinois, the Blackhawks made the playoffs with Murray contributing seven points per game. During the 1950-51 season he played fifty-one games with the Waterloo Hawks of the National Professional Basketball League.

His playing days complete, Wier looked for new challenges. Hired by East High in Waterloo, Murray began a Hall of Fame coaching career. In 1954 he took the Trojans to the state tournament. After a first round victory, they met Wier's alma mater, Muscatine. The Muskies proved to be too much, wining 66-50 on their way to the championship. His 1974 East squad made it to the state tournament, putting three wins together to claim the championship. Following the season Murray retired as coach, staying on as Athletic Director.

The man with the nicknames "Rampaging Redhead" and "Wizard Wier" is in both the IHSAA player and coaches Hall of Fame, the Quad Cities Hall of Fame, East High Hall of Fame, and selected to the All-Time Big Ten team. Not bad for a little guy playing in a big man's sport.

92 – Jon Lieber

Hometown: Council Bluffs

Lieber began his high school baseball career as an outfielder before moving to the mound as a senior at Abraham Lincoln in Council Bluffs. As a walk-on at Iowa Western Community College it took nearly a year before he was used and then only as a relief pitcher. During his sophomore year he helped the team to the Junior College World Series. Transferring to the University of South Alabama, Jon became a starting pitcher, twice leading the Jags to NCAA tournament appearances. A two-time All-Conference pick, Lieber was the 1992 Sun Belt Conference Player of the Year and selected third team All-America.

Drafted by the Kansas City Royals in the second round, Jon spent a year in their minor league system before a trade brought him to Pittsburgh. In 1994 he made his major league debut, a 1-0 loss to the Phillies. In the five years Jon pitched for the Pirates, he had just one season with a winning record. In December of 1998 he was on the move to the Chicago Cubs.

His first year as a Cub was much like that in Pittsburgh; he finished with an 11-12 record. Year two brought a winning record and then in 2001 he had a career year. Jon posted a 20-6 record and was selected to play in the 2001 All-Star game. The reason for the sudden improvement was his gain of pitch control. He became one of the league leaders in fewest walks per nine innings.

Lieber sustained an arm injury in 2002 that required surgery. As a free agent, there was doubt any club would take a chance by signing him. The New York Yankees took that chance and after sitting out the 2003 season, Jon pitched in 2004. After a 7-7 start, he rattled off a 7-1 record in his last eight decisions, helping the Yankees win the division title. He signed with Philadelphia in 2005 and led the league with thirty-five games started. He ranked in the top ten of pitching control statistics and finished fifth with seventeen wins.

Major League Pitching Record

12 Seasons	W	L	G	IP	H	ER	BB	SO	ERA
Career	129	115	361	2073.1	2238	981	394	1472	4.26

93 – Kip Janvrin

Hometown: Panora

A multiple sport athlete at Panora-Linden High School, Janvrin blossomed as a decathlete during his time at Simpson College, winning three NCAA Division III championships. In 1988 he also captured NCAA titles in the 400-meter hurdles and pole vault. He still holds four Simpson College school records. One of the most decorated Division III athletes, Kip was elected to the NCAA Division III Track and Field Hall of Fame in 2004.

After graduation he continued to compete in decathlons, becoming a force on the national and international level. From 1989 through 2003, he was nationally ranked and earned a spot on the 2000 Olympic team by finishing third at the trials. Janvrin's longevity is unprecedented in U.S. decathlon history. He established a world record for career decathlon wins and an American record for most career decathlons scoring over 8,000 points.

The Drake Relays has been a place for Kip to showcase his ability, having won the decathlon an amazing fourteen times. He won nine consecutive titles from 1995 though 2003, including a Drake Relays and Drake Stadium record 8,198 points in 1996. In 1998 he was inducted into the Drake Relays Hall of Fame.

Janvrin has coached track at Central Missouri State University in Warrensburg since 1990. He has served, with West Liberty native Kirk Peterson, as co-head coach since 1998. In 2002 the duo were named USTCA National Indoor Coaches of the Year.

Career Highlights:

1993 - 4th at USA Championship - ranked #5 in U.S.
1994 - 3rd at USA Championship - ranked #10 in world , #3 U.S.
1995 - Pan American Games champion - ranked #5 in U.S.
1996 - 4th at Olympic Trials - ranked #4 in U.S.
1999 - 4th at USA Champs - ranked #5 in U.S.
2000 - 21st at 2000 Olympics, 3rd at Olympic Trials
2001 - USA Outdoor champion
2002 - 10th at USA Outdoors

94 – Johnny Lindell

Hometown: Winfield

Born in Colorado, Lindell's family moved to Iowa, settling in the Winfield area. After graduation Johnny headed for the University of Southern California, playing on the Trojan baseball team.

In 1940 the New York Yankees signed Lindell to a professional contract, sending him to pitch for their minor league team in Kansas City. He had a good year, completing the season with eighteen wins. In 1941 Johnny had a tremendous season with the Yank's top minor league team in Newark, New Jersey. After posting a record of 23-4, the *Sporting News* named him their minor league Player of the Year.

His major league career started in 1942 when he was a little-used relief pitcher. Maybe as a result of the wartime shortage of players the Yankees converted Lindell into an outfielder in 1943 and he responded by leading the league in triples. He experienced the thrill of an All-Star selection and tied a major league record with four consecutive doubles. The Yankees made it to the World Series, and Johnny had only one hit in nine at bats. However, that one hit ignited an eighth inning rally as the Yankees rallied to win game three and eventually the series.

With the return of Joe DiMaggio from military service, Lindell's role was reduced to a utility player. In nine full seasons with New York, Johnny played on three World Series championship teams, leading the 1947 squad by hitting .500 and driving in seven runs in the series.

After a trade to the St. Louis Cardinals and then his release, he played in the Pacific League returning to pitching. Utilizing a knuckleball, he won twenty-four games and was named the league's Player of the Year. Following a call-up to the Pittsburgh Pirates in 1953, Johnny had trouble controlling the knuckleball leading to a league high 139 batters walked. Traded to Philadelphia, Lindell finished his career used mainly as a pinch hitter for the Phillies.

Major League Pitching Record

12 Seasons	G	AB	R	H	2B	3B	HR	RBI	AVG
Career	854	2795	401	762	124	48	72	404	.273

95 – Tom Farmer

Hometown: Davenport

Farmer was born in Cedar Rapids where he played football, baseball and basketball at Wilson High School. As a running back, he earned third team All-State recognition in 1938.

A three-year letter winner at the University of Iowa, he starred both as left halfback in the "Notre Dame" system and as quarterback in the T-formation. Farmer led Iowa to a six win season in 1942 and garnered team MVP and Big Ten first team honors. The season's pinnacle was the homecoming contest with nationally top-rated Wisconsin. Five Hawkeyes played every minute of the game including Farmer. It was Tom who pulled off the game's biggest play by connecting with Bill Burket for the winning touchdown.

The Cleveland Browns made Tom their second round pick in the 1943 draft. He never had the opportunity to play for the Browns. Instead he spent nearly three years as a First Lieutenant with the Marines during World War II. Stationed on Guam, he was wounded in the line of duty and decorated with honors.

Back in the states and recovered from his war wounds, Tom became a member of the 1946 Los Angeles Rams. As a running back and defensive back, Tom saw limited playing time. In 1947 he was traded to the Washington Redskins. During his two seasons in Washington, Tom saw limited action on offense because of his excellence on defense. In 1947 he led the team with six interceptions.

NFL Record

			Rushing			Receiving		
Year	Team	G	ATT	YDS	TD	REC	YDS	TD
1946	LA Rams	8	28	90	1	6	17	0
1947	Wash	10	15	29	1	8	137	0
1948	Wash	9	52	188	1	12	148	2
Career		27	95	307	3	26	302	2

96 – Nile Kinnick

Hometown: Adel

There are some with the belief that had Nile Kinnick not perished in an airplane crash during World War II, he would have been elected our nation's President. Following his Iowa career, Kinnick chose to go to law school and join the Naval Air Corps Reserve. Mechanical failure on a training flight caused his plane to crash into the ocean and his body was never recovered. Iowa and America lost a great leader. The Big Ten Conference honors Kinnick yearly; his likeness is on the face of the coin tossed at the start of every conference football game.

The grandson of a former governor, Nile was born on July 9, 1918, in Adel. A star athlete in football and basketball at Adel High School, he was named to the 1934 football All-State fifth team. As a junior Nile scored more than a third of his team's points in basketball. In the days of low scoring, he accumulated more than 1,000 career points. He also played on an American Legion baseball team, catching for future Hall of Fame pitcher Bob Feller.

After his senior year at Benson High in Omaha, Nile set off for Iowa City to pursue academic and football dreams. At the time Iowa football was in the conference basement. During his first two seasons the team's record was 2-13-1, but then entered new coach, Mason City native Dr. Eddie Anderson. The 1939 season became one of mythical proportions. With limited space, I cannot due justice to even highlights. Any sports fan, and especially Hawkeye fans, should read one of the books chronicling the "Ironman" season, so named due to the number of two-way players used by Iowa throughout the year. During one portion of the season Kinnick played 402 consecutive minutes until being sidelined with a separated shoulder.

With average size and speed, Nile excelled when the game was in the balance and leadership was a premium. As a punter or passer, a runner or leader, he willed Iowa to victories. He threw the game wining pass against Indiana and a late touchdown pass to upend Wisconsin. In the 7-6 upset of Notre Dame he delivered sixteen punts for 731 yards, including a sixty-three yard effort to seal the victory. He accounted for 107 of Iowa's 130 season points. Everyone's All-American, Nile was the recipient of the 1939 Heisman Trophy and delivered a most eloquent acceptance speech.

97 – Bob Feller

Hometown: Van Meter

Van Meter native Bob Feller is one of the major league's all-time great pitchers. With a passion for baseball instilled by his father, Bob played whenever he had the chance. As a high school and American Legion pitcher he dominated his peers, and by the age of sixteen he was pitching for a semi-professional team in Des Moines. It was there that a Cleveland Indian scout noticed Bob, signing him to a contract during his junior year of high school.

While his classmates spent the summer of 1936 on vacation, Feller pitched for the Indians. For the season he posted five victories and tied the major league record by striking out seventeen batters in a game. He returned to Van Meter for his senior year, playing on the basketball team, then left for Cleveland before getting a chance to participate in the graduation ceremony.

A nine time All-Star, known for a blazing fastball, Bob was a strike out pitcher and soon acquired the nickname " Rapid Robert." In 1939 he led the league with a 24-9 record, then topped those numbers by winning a career high twenty-seven games in 1940. With twenty-five wins in 1941 it looked as if Bob was on his way to establishing new records for career wins and strike-outs. That changed three days after the bombing of Pearl Harbor. Bob enlisted in the Navy giving up four prime baseball years for service to his country. It is realistic to believe his career numbers would have an additional 100 wins and 1,000 strikeouts.

Upon his return to the major leagues, Bob picked up right where he left, leading the league in wins and strikeouts. In 1948 the Indians made it to the World Series. Bob lost both games he pitched but the team won the championship. After retiring in 1956 the Indians retired his uniform number and in 1962 Bob was elected to Baseball's Hall of Fame.

Major League Pitching Record

18 Years	W	L	G	SV	IP	SO	ERA
Career	266	162	570	21	3827	2581	3.25

98 – Walt McCredie

Hometown: Sioux City

McCredie was born in Manchester but grew up in Sioux City. Playing baseball on their favorite sandlot, Walt and his friends coined the phrase "Charley Horse" after an old crippled horse in the adjacent pasture. When one of them limped with an injury, the others razzed him about looking like "Old Charley Horse."

Walt began his professional career in 1895 spending eight seasons in the minors before making it to the major league in 1903. Playing for Brooklyn he hit .324 in fifty-six games, but remarkably it was his only season in the major league.

After the season Walt spent time in Oregon, then in 1905 became part owner of the Portland team in the Pacific Coast League with his uncle, Judge W.W. McCredie. The team became a family operation with the Judge as president and Walt as playing manager. At the turn of the century the Pacific Coast League was classified a minor league, but the caliber of play was on the level of the majors. McCredie turned the team into a contender, winning five league titles before selling his share of the team after the 1921 season.

The team's first championship came in 1906. Improved on the field, the Beavers won the pennant with a 114-58 record and finished twenty-one games ahead of second place Los Angeles. Walt, playing right field, was Portland's second leading hitter, batting .305 with twenty-eight stolen bases, good for fourth in the league. Following the 1910 season, he retired as a player and devoted full attention to the role of manager.

In 1922 Walt managed the Seattle team, then stayed away from the game until 1934. At that time he was coaxed into a return to Portland but his health began to fail. The club planned a night to honor McCredie as he was considered the "founding father" of the Beavers, having managed and played with the team during its inception. Unfortunately the game became a memorial as he passed away prior to the event.

Major League Hitting Record

Year	Team	G	AB	R	H	2B	3B	HR	RBI	BA
1903	BRO	56	213	40	69	5	0	0	20	.324

99 – Harris Coggeshall

Hometown: Des Moines

Many of today's top tennis players use a two-hand backhand; some have even used a two-hand forehand. That wasn't the case in the early part of the century when Des Moines' Harris Coggeshall used two hands because he couldn't swing hard enough with one. He was about ten years old at the time, making his competitive debut in a junior tournament in Boston.

By the time he was seventeen he was city and state champion. In today's sport climate, Coggeshall would more than likely move to either Florida or California to pursue a tennis career. At the very least a player with budding talent would attend a college with a big time program; instead Harris chose to attend Grinnell College. His talent led him to claim the Missouri Valley Conference singles title in 1927, 1928, and 1929. Each of those years Grinnell also claimed the team title over schools such as Oklahoma, Kansas, Iowa State, and Missouri. Teaming with George Struble, Harris added the 1928 doubles title. Tennis was not his only sport; he played on the basketball team, serving as captain.

During the time he was at Grinnell and at Harvard Law School, Harris played in tournaments throughout Iowa, the Midwest, and at the national level. Once in singles and three times in doubles he made it to the national championship match only to fall just short of winning. He advanced as far as anyone could who put education and a professional career ahead of an athletic career.

At age twenty-six, with his college degree from Grinnell and a law degree from Harvard, he restricted his tournament play when he began the practice of law. He played enough to win eight city championships and an equal number of state titles. Handball and squash soon became his sports of choice, winning state titles in handball and topping the local competition in squash.

Coggeshall played many of the top players of his time, losing a tight match to the famed Bill Tilden and beating the likes of Ellsworth Vines and Frank Parker. Had he given tennis full attention, in all likelihood he would have been one of the sport's top players.

100 – Joe Laws

Hometown: Colfax

Laws played football and baseball, and ran track for Colfax High School. Football was his specialty, and his high school career included a ninety-two yard punt return for a touchdown against Des Moines Lincoln High School in 1927.

Joe was a three-year letter winner for the Hawkeyes. Following his senior season he was selected as All-Big Ten quarterback and Big Ten MVP. As a second team All-American, Laws led the Hawkeyes to a five and three record, then in the spring would play on the baseball team. He was chosen to play in the East/West game, calling signals for the East. The following summer, the fans selected him as the quarterback for the college All-Stars, helping the All-Stars play to a 0-0 tie with the Chicago Bears. In 1991 Joe was elected to the National Iowa Varsity Club Athletic Hall of Fame.

Professional football was his next calling and Joe signed with Green Bay. One of the most versatile backs in Packer history, Joe played both running back positions along with fullback and quarterback. The NFL utilized one-platoon football, and on defense he played as a defensive back. Joe was always ready to do whatever needed to help the team win a championship: a feat accomplished three times during his career. At the age of thirty-four, Joe played in his most memorable game when the Packers went against the New York Giants in a playoff game. He personally took charge of the defeat of the Giants, carrying the ball thirteen times for seventy-two yards to lead all ball carriers. He also set a league record with three pass interceptions.

At the time of his retirement, Joe ranked number five on the Packers' all-time scoring list and number three in NFL career interceptions. He was instrumental in the organization of the Packer Alumni and in 1972 was elected to the Packers Hall of Fame.

NFL Rushing/Receiving Record

12 Seasons	G	ATT	YDS	TD	REC	YDS	TD
Career	120	470	1932	9	79	1041	9

101 – Dennis Gibson

Hometown: Ankeny

The San Diego Chargers were in the 1995 Super Bowl because of the play of Dennis Gibson. In the League Championship game against the favored Pittsburgh Steelers, the Chargers were ahead late in the game as the Steelers marched down the field, apparently for the go-ahead touchdown. With under a minute remaining, the Steelers were down to their last play, a fourth and goal play from inside the ten yard line. Barry Foster was Gibson's assignment and Neal O'Donnell tried to rifle the ball to a seemingly open Foster. At the last second Gibson got his fingers on the ball, knocking it harmlessly to the ground. With that incompletion a Super Bowl berth was a reality for the Chargers, just an inch from a devastating loss.

Gibson had been an eighth round pick of the Detroit Lions in 1985 following an outstanding career at Iowa State, including team MVP and Knudson Award winner for defensive excellence. Dennis had played as a linebacker for Ankeny High School and was named second team All-State following his senior season.

Success followed in the NFL when he became the first rookie to lead the Lions in tackles. In his seven years with Detroit, he started every game he played and ranks ninth on the Lions' career tackle list. Following the 1993 season Gibson became a free agent, signing with the Chargers. After three seasons in San Diego, his playing days has come to an end.

NFL Defensive Record

Year	Team	G	SKS	FR	INT	TD	TKL
1987	Detroit	12	1	0	1	0	82
1988	Detroit	16	0.5	1	0	0	116
1989	Detroit	6	0	3	1	0	29
1990	Detroit	11	0	1	0	0	68
1991	Detroit	16	0	0	0	0	63
1992	Detroit	16	0	0	0	0	62
1993	San Diego	15	1	1	1	0	62
1994	San Diego	16	0	0	0	0	68
1995	San Diego	13	0	0	0	0	52
Career		121	2.5	6	3	0	602

102 – Hal Trosky

Hometown: Norway

Born in one of Iowa's baseball hotbeds, the town of Norway, Hal Trojovsky shortened his name to Trosky when he signed to play professional ball. After starring on the high school team, Hal signed with the Cedar Rapids Bunnies in 1931. He played with minor league teams in Dubuque and Burlington prior to making his last stop at Toledo, Ohio, before a late season call to the Indians in 1933.

Trosky batted .330 as a rookie in 1934, displaying power with thirty-five homers, forty-five doubles, and 142 RBI. His 364 total bases set the major league record for rookies. In the second game of a Memorial Day doubleheader against the White Sox, Hal belted three successive home runs. His 1936 season was considered truly outstanding as he led the league in total bases, runs batted in, and extra base hits. In addition to those power numbers, Hal put together a twenty-eight game hitting streak as he hit for a .342 average.

After the 1941 season, Trosky announced an early retirement, due to migraine headaches. Returning to Iowa he worked on the farm and in a factory. In 1943 he decided to return to baseball. He was sold to the White Sox and hit just ten home runs in 1944. Sitting out a season, he played in 1946, then became a White Sox scout.

Throughout his time in the majors Trosky was always among the league leaders in home runs and runs batted in. Unfortunately, Hal played during the same time as Hall of Fame first basemen Jimmy Foxx, Lou Gehrig, Hank Greenberg, Bill Terry and Jim Bottomley. That made it difficult to get deserved recognition and the Indian pitchers, including Iowan Bob Feller, received more local press. Additionally, Hal's reputation was tarnished when he was falsely accused of leading a player revolt against the Indians' manager during the 1940 season.

Major League Hitting Record

11 seasons	G	AB	R	H	2B	3B	HR	RBI	AVG
Career	1347	5161	835	1561	331	58	228	1012	.302

103 – Nate Kaeding

Hometown: Iowa City

Kaeding is one of the top kickers in Iowa prep history. He holds all the kicking and punting records at Iowa City West High School. When he ended his career he was the state's all-time leader in points for a season, career points, and career points after touchdown. The West High football team won back-to-back state titles his junior and senior seasons. As a basketball player, he was a starter on the Trojan squad that won the state title. Also, Nate was a three year starter on the soccer team. When the 1999 state championship game went to a shoot-out, it was Nate's goal that provided the victory for West.

A scoring weapon during his four years with the Hawkeyes, Nate established Big Ten Conference career and season kicking points records. Numerous times he was selected as conference Special Team Player of the Week.

Kaeding's College Honors

2000: Third team Freshman All-American

2001: Academic All-Big Ten, Honorable Mention All-Big Ten
Iowa Special Team Player of the Year

2002: Lou Groza award winner, consensus All-American
First-team All-Big Ten, first-team Academic All-American
Verizon second-team Academic All-American

2003: First-team All-American, Lou Groza Award finalist
First-team All-Big Ten, first-team Academic All-American

Drafted by the San Diego Chargers in round three, Nate set a team rookie record by scoring 114 points, the leading total for all NFL rookies. Included in those points was a game-winning, forty-three yard field goal against the Kansas City Chiefs. During the 2005 season Nate continued to be a valuable asset to the team with his kicking consistency.

NFL Kicking Record

Year	Team	G	XP	FG	PTS
2004	San Diego	16	54/55	20/25	114
2005	San Diego	16	49/49	21/24	112
Career		32	103/104	41/49	226

104 – Wally Hilgenberg

Hometown: Wilton Junction

As a student at Wilton Junction High School, Wally played football, basketball, baseball, and ran track. Football was his sport of choice even though he was not heavily recruited. He landed at the University of Iowa and intentions were to have him play quarterback. Instead he made a move to guard and linebacker in his sophomore season. He became a fine player, earning third-team All-American and first-team All-Big Ten honors, and playing in four post-season bowl games.

Hilgenberg had the distinction of being drafted by Denver in round eight of the 1964 AFL draft and in round four of the NFL draft by the Detroit Lions. He played three years with the Lions before sitting out the 1967 season due to injuries. The Pittsburgh Steelers acquired him but sold him to the Vikings before the start of the 1968 season. Stepping into the starting linebacker position, he played the next twelve seasons in Minnesota. Wally had the privilege of playing in four Super Bowls with Minnesota. Unfortunately, the Vikings were unable to win a championship.

NFL Defensive Record

Year	Team	G	INT	FR	TD
1964	Detroit	14	0	0	0
1965	Detroit	13	0	0	0
1966	Detroit	14	0	0	0
1968	Minnesota	14	0	0	0
1969	Minnesota	14	0	0	0
1970	Minnesota	14	2	0	0
1971	Minnesota	14	2	0	0
1972	Minnesota	14	1	1	1
1973	Minnesota	13	1	1	1
1974	Minnesota	13	1	0	0
1975	Minnesota	14	1	0	0
1976	Minnesota	14	0	0	0
1977	Minnesota	11	0	0	0
1978	Minnesota	15	0	0	0
1979	Minnesota	8	0	0	0
Career		199	8	2	2

105 – Roger Craig

Hometown: Davenport

An outstanding athlete at Davenport Central High School, Roger wrestled, ran track, and played football. As a running back he earned Elite Team All-State and All-American recognition. Recruited by many schools, he chose to follow his brother Curtis to Nebraska. Sharing running duties with Heisman Trophy winner Mike Rozier, his statistics as a Cornhusker were not very impressive. Never the less, NFL scouts understood his contribution to the team and saw potential as a runner.

Drafted in the second round by the San Francisco Forty-Niners in 1983, Craig quickly became a part of the offense as he rushed for 725 yards his rookie year. The Forty-Niners employed a type of offense that included controlled passing, meaning the backs were the primary targets on many plays. In 1985 he became the first player to gain 1,000 yards both rushing and receiving in a single season. In 1990 Roger became the first running back to reach 500 career receptions. The team was also very successful. During his eight years with the Forty-Niners, Roger collected three Super Bowl Championships.

In 1991 Roger became a Plan B free agent, leaving San Francisco and signing with the Los Angeles Raiders. His one season with the Raiders netted him a team leading 590 rushing yards. In 1992 he signed with the Vikings and was reunited with former Forty-Niner assistant coach and Iowa grad, Dennis Green. Green knew the value of having Craig on the squad even though he was beyond his most productive years. In the two seasons Roger was with Minnesota, he carried the ball just 143 times for 535 yards, numbers he usually put up in a half a season during his prime.

Roger played in 114 consecutive games before a knee injury sidelined him in 1990. His durability came from the demanding off-season training he would go through each year. His characteristic high knee running style and ability to run through tackles resulted from the dedication of those off-season workouts.

NFL Rushing/Receiving Record

11 seasons	G	ATT	YDS	TD	REC	YDS	TD
Career	165	1991	8189	56	566	4911	17

106 – Casey Wiegmann

Hometown: Parkersburg

Casey typifies many of the state's high school athletes. He had a dream of playing football for the Iowa Hawkeyes and worked until the dream became a reality. It also takes size and ability to play collegiately, and he possessed both. For a guy his size Casey has tremendous speed, running on his high school 400-meter and 800-meter relay teams. On the gridiron Wiegmann was selected to the Elite All-State Team and Super Prep All-Region as a defensive lineman in 1990. He also served as the team's punter and place kicker at Parkersburg High School, whose team finished as runner up for the Class 1A title in 1990.

A three year starter at center for Iowa, Casey was a team captain his senior year. He was selected to the Honorable Mention Big Ten team by both the coaches and media following his senior season and played in both the Hula and East/West Shrine Bowl games.

Undrafted, Casey signed with the Indianapolis Colts in 1996 and was assigned to their practice squad for the first nine games. Before game ten, he was signed by the New York Jets and was activated for games twelve and sixteen, but didn't play in either game. In 1997 he played in three games with the Jets, and then was released in mid-season. Immediately signed by the Chicago Bears, he appeared in just one game the remainder of the year.

From 1998 through 2000, Casey was with Chicago, starting at center a good portion of the time. The Bears were not very good, winning a total of fifteen games in those three seasons. Following the 2000 season, he became a free agent and signed with the Kansas City Chiefs, a team that had playoff potential. He stepped in as the starting center and became a key component in an offensive line that is one of the best units in the NFL. The Chiefs were the top-scoring team in both the 2003 and 2004 seasons, and a big reason was the offensive line.

NFL Game Record

1997 NYJ: 3 G ChiB: 1 G	**1998** ChiB: 16 G	**1999** ChiB: 16G
2000 ChiB: 16 G	**2001** KC: 15 G	**2002** KC: 16 G
2003 KC: 16 G	**2004** KC: 16 G	**2005** KC: 16G

Career: 131 G

107 – Stan Bahnsen

Hometown: Council Bluffs

An outstanding pitcher for Council Bluffs' Abraham Lincoln High School, Bahnsen attended the University of Nebraska and played only one season of baseball. The New York Yankees selected Stan in the fourth round of the 1965 amateur draft and assigned him to their team in Columbus, Georgia. After pitching a no-hit game for the Toledo Mudhens the Yankees brought Bahnsen to the major league team late in the 1966 season. Appearing in four games, Stan earned a win and a save. He spent the following season at the organization's top farm team in Syracuse, pitching a perfect game along the way.

When the big league club broke camp in the spring of 1968, Stan was on the roster, becoming a member of the starting rotation. During that rookie campaign he started thirty-seven games, posted a 17-12 record, had an ERA of 2.06, struck out 162 batters, and was named the American League Rookie of the Year. Stan's performance dropped off the following season, and after two additional mediocre years he was traded to the Chicago White Sox. With twenty-one, eighteen, and twelve wins the first three seasons in Chicago, it looked as if the Yankees gave up on Stan too soon.

Midway through the 1975 season, Bahnsen was traded to Oakland. He continued to work as a starting pitcher until a trade to Montreal in 1977. In his final five seasons, Stan was used out of the bullpen, at times as the closer, but more often in long relief. He appeared in one game for the Expos during the 1981 National League Division Series, pitching an inning and a third of scoreless relief. Stan finished his major league career in 1982 by splitting time with the California Angels and Philadelphia Phillies.

In 1989 he put on the spikes again when he played for the Gulf Coast Sun in the Senior Professional Baseball Association, a winter league based in Florida for players thirty-five years of age or older.

Major League Pitching Record

16 Seasons	G	W	L	SV	IP	H	ERA
Career	574	146	149	20	2528.7	2440	3.61

108 – T.J. Rubley

Hometown: Davenport

"Sacrificial Ram?" read the headline in the *Des Moines Register* on October 24, 1993, as Davenport native Theron Joseph "T.J." Rubley prepared to make his first NFL start for the Los Angeles Rams. Rubley, a ninth round pick in the 1992 draft, with very little NFL experience, was getting his first start against the powerful San Francisco Forty-Niners, thus the headline. Coach Chuck Knox decided to start T.J. in an attempt to energize the offense. The game did not go well for Rubley or the Rams as the Forty-Niners coasted to a 40 to 17 win. For the day T.J. was fifteen of twenty-six passing with one touchdown, but he also threw two interceptions. For the season he threw eight touchdowns.

Rubley's 1994 season was lost to an elbow injury, then released by the Rams in 1995 before signing with the Green Bay Packers. He played in one game, throwing an interception and calling a fourth down audible that failed. Coach Mike Holmgren was not pleased with that decision, so T.J. was released. Signed by the Denver Broncos, Rubley was allocated to the World League of American Football in 1997, playing with the Rhein Fire. He was the league's leading passer and named Offensive Player of the Year, while guiding his team to the World Bowl.

In 1998 T.J. played in his third professional league when he played a final season with the Winnipeg and Hamilton teams of the Canadian Football League.

Over a span of eighteen years, there were four Rubley brothers to play quarterback for Davenport West. T.J. was the last, earning All-State and All-America mention after completing 253 of 490 passes for 4,009 yards and thirty-eight touchdowns in three seasons. He played for the University of Tulsa, where he set team records for passing completions, attempts, yards, and touchdowns.

Professional Passing Record

5 Seasons	ATT	CMP	YDS	TD	INT
Career	585	384	4496	24	27

109 – Ed Podolak

Hometown: Atlantic

In the mid-1960s the sports teams at Atlantic High School were filled with great athletes. Ed Podolak was one of those players and he had aspirations of playing beyond high school. Some had doubts he would succeed at a division one school, but he became a standout for the Iowa Hawkeyes. Dreams and the desire to accomplish the dream are as important as having the natural ability.

As a Hawkeye, Ed excelled as a runner and a passer. During his sophomore and junior seasons he played quarterback, passing for over 1,000 yards in each season. As a senior he moved to running back and gained a team-leading 937 yards. His 286 yards against Northwestern in 1968 set an Iowa single game record that stood until 1997. Podolak is one of two Hawkeyes with over 1,000 career yards in both rushing and passing. As you look at the career top ten lists, you will find Ed Podolak listed in rushing, passing, and total offense. Rewards for a fine senior season came with All-Big Ten recognition and playing in three all-star bowls: the East/West Shrine, the Hula, and the Tribune All-Star.

His dream of playing in the NFL came to fruition as he was drafted in round two of the 1969 draft by the Kansas City Chiefs. He was on the Super Bowl championship team of 1969, but did not have any carries until the 1970 season when he gained a team leading 749 yards. For the next three years Ed was the Chiefs' leading ground gainer and added to the offense with his receiving skills. In one of the most memorable NFL games, he had 350 total yards in the playoff loss to the Miami Dolphins on Christmas Day of 1971. In 1989 the Chiefs honored Ed with election to their Hall of Fame.

After his playing days, Ed undertook business opportunities in Colorado. For a number of years he has been a part of Iowa football as an analyst for the Hawkeye radio broadcasts.

NFL Rushing / Receiving Record

9 Seasons	G	ATT	YDS	TD	REC	YDS	TD
Career	104	1157	4451	34	288	2456	6

110 – Dazzy Vance

Hometown: Orient

Dazzy Vance didn't play his first full major league season until age thirty-one. Three previous stints with major-league clubs produced a 0-4 record and an earned run average of over 4.00.

Throwing a blazing fastball, Vance began his minor league professional career in 1912. He had problems with his control until 1914 when he posted a 26-12 record. The Pittsburgh Pirates took notice, giving Vance a chance in the big leagues in 1915. His control problems returned and he was sent back to the minors. The Yankees gave him a shot in 1918, and he stuck for a while until his elbow became inflamed. The injury may have been a blessing as he developed a curve ball and gained control of the fastball.

Fortunately the Brooklyn Dodgers gave him one more chance. After ten years in professional baseball, he joined the Dodgers in 1922 and became the league's strikeout leader each of the next seven seasons, as well as its MVP in 1924. Dazzy's 1924 season was one for the ages. He earned pitching's triple crown: compiling a 28-6 record, posting a 2.16 ERA and striking out an impressive 262 batters, all were league leading totals. A teammate struck out 135 batters, finishing second, 127 whiffs behind Vance. He accounted for eight percent of all strikeouts in the league that year. No pitcher in history can claim such strikeout dominance. In fact, he was so dominant that he edged St. Louis' second baseman Rogers Hornsby for the Most Valuable Player award, despite Hornsby's .424 batting average, a twentieth century record.

In February of 1933, Vance was traded to the St. Louis Cardinals. Having lost something off his fastball, he appeared in only nineteen games for the 1934 "Gashouse Gang," but he did pitch in one game of the Cardinals' winning World Series. In the inning and a third he pitched, three of the four outs were strikeouts. Back with Brooklyn in 1935, Dazzy finished his career working out of the bullpen. Twenty years later he was elected to the Baseball Hall of Fame.

Major League Pitching Record

16 Seasons	W	L	G	SV	IP	H	ER	SO	ERA
Career	197	140	442	11	2966.7	2809	1068	2045	3.24

111 – Fred Clarke

Hometown: Winterset

The Winterset-born Clarke may have been the greatest player-manager in professional baseball history. As a player he amassed 2,703 career hits and totaled 1,602 managerial wins. Elected to the Baseball Hall of Fame as a player, he could have entered as a manager as well.

As a two-year old the family moved to Kansas, returning to Iowa five years later. After the family settled in the Des Moines area, Fred carried newspapers for Ed Barrow. Barrow had organized a ball team and Clarke soon was one of the players. Barrow would go on to become the General Manager of the New York Yankees and Fred became a professional player. His early days as a pro were spent on teams that were financial failures, often folding in mid-season. That changed in 1894 when his contract became the property of the Louisville Colonels, then a team in the major leagues.

In his first game for the Colonels, Fred went five for five at the plate, the only player to accomplish this fete. He was named player-manager in 1897, batting .407 and stealing sixty bases. The Louisville team wasn't able to make it financially; thus in 1900 they dissolved, merging with the Pittsburgh organization. Clarke continued as player-manager, leading the Pirates to the first World Series in 1903, only to lose to the Red Sox in five games. Fred led them back to the Series in 1909, this time beating Detroit in an exciting seven game Series.

Fred stayed with the Pirates through the 1915 season but rarely played after 1911. The team continued to finish in the top division but did not return to the World Series under Clarke's guidance. Near the close of the 1915 season, he was honored at Forbes Field with "Fred Clarke Day". After ten years of retirement, Clarke was coaxed into a return to the Pirates as a coach. The following year he became vice-president and assistant manager. After the 1926 season he returned to his farm in Kansas, closing his baseball career.

Major League Record

21 Seasons	G	AB	R	H	2B	3B	HR	RBI	BA
Career	2242	8568	1619	2672	361	220	67	1015	.312

112 – Matt Bullard

Hometown: West Des Moines

Playing for Valley High School of West Des Moines Matt earned first team All-State honors in 1985. He accepted a basketball scholarship from the University of Colorado, earning All-Big Eight freshman team honors. Matt became one of the top players for the Buffaloes, but following his sophomore season he decided to transfer to the University of Iowa. As a Hawkeye he played on teams with more depth so he didn't score as much, but the team made it to the NCAA tournament. Twice during his college career he represented the United States in the World University Games, playing on the silver medal squad in 1987 and winning a gold medal in 1989.

In 1990 Matt was drafted in the third round by Yakima of the CBA but was not selected during the NBA draft. Given a NBA opportunity as a free agent with the Houston, Matt began the first of two stints with the Rockets. He played as a reserve on the 1993-94 team that won the NBA Championship. The following season he played for PAOK Thessaloniki of Greece in the Euroleague. Back in the NBA in 1996, Bullard played a year for Atlanta before re-signing with Houston.

Matt was known for his ability to shoot from the outside, particularly the three-point shot, and was given the nickname "Air Bull" because of the height on his shot. He set a Rocket franchise record for three-point percentage by shooting .446 during the 1999-2000 season. After five seasons in Houston, he was traded to Charlotte where he played his final season.

In the spring of 2005 Matt competed along with five other former NBA players for ESPN's "Dream Job." The winner received a contract to provide commentary on ESPN broadcasts of NBA games. Surviving a series of elimination rounds, he made the finals, only to finish as runner-up. That experience did lead to a job as an analyst for Rockets' television broadcasts during the 2005-06 season.

NBA Record

11 Seasons	G	FG	3P	FT	RB	AST	PTS
Career	615	1215	599	241	1223	535	3270

113 – Zach Johnson

Hometown: Cedar Rapids

Zach was born in Iowa City and attended Regis High School in Cedar Rapids. He was the number two scorer on the Regis golf team that captured the 1992 State Class 3-A Championship and 1993 State Fall Class 4-A runner-up trophy. Attending Drake University, he earned four golf letters and led the Bulldogs to the Missouri Valley Conference championships in 1997 and 1998.

Johnson played the first two seasons of his professional career on the Prairie Golf Tour collecting three wins and finishing third on the money list in 1999. After struggling as a rookie on the Nationwide Tour in 2000, Zach spent the 2001 and 2002 seasons on the Hooters Tour. In 2001 he won the final three regular-season events and was named the tour's Player of the Year.

Back on the Nationwide in 2003, Johnson put together a record breaking year. Making the cut in nineteen of twenty tournaments, he was named the Tour Player of the Year. He won two tournaments, set a tour single-season earnings record, and established a record with nine top three finishes. The final reward for his incredible season was qualification for the 2004 PGA Tour.

In the thirteenth event of his PGA rookie season Zach was leading the Bell South Tournament going into the final round. Holding a slim lead and with the pressure to win mounting, he was able to par the last three holes to claim victory. He capped the year as part of the winning team in the inaugural Tommy Bahama Classic, a four-man challenge between U.S. and international golfers under the age of thirty.

Zach played well during the 2005 and 2006 seasons. While he did not win a tournament, he did earn enough points to qualify for the United States Ryder Cup team. Held semi-annually, the Ryder Cup matches the U.S. against a team comprised of golfers from Europe. In recent history these matches have been very competitive and with four Ryder Cup rookies the U.S. team was considered a long-shot to claim victory. Zach played in each format of the Cup's competition including four-ball, foursomes, and singles. Playing well considering the enormity of the event, he earned one and a halve points of the U.S. total of nine and a halve points as the team fell to the European team.

114 – Don Norton

Hometown: Anamosa

After a fifth team All-State high school career at Anamosa High School, Norton had to decide whether to play football at the University of Iowa or Coe College. He chose the Hawks and became one of the last two-way players at Iowa. As a tight end Don had exceptional speed and led the team in receptions for two seasons. First team All-Big Ten his senior season, Don had first team All-America recognition his junior year and second team following his senior. He served as team captain for the 1959 season and at the conclusion of the season he was voted team MVP. These are quite impressive accomplishments for a player not many people knew about when he first showed up in Iowa City.

After representing the Hawks in the East/West Shrine and Senior Bowl, Don was a fifth round choice of the Philadelphia Eagles in the 1960 draft. In the inaugural AFL draft, Minneapolis selected Don with their first pick. Minneapolis was offered a NFL franchise, relinquishing the rights of their drafted players. San Diego signed Don and he spent eight seasons playing for the Chargers. Sure-handed with good speed, Don became a four-time All-Pro as he caught almost anything he got his hands on. The Chargers were one of the league's top teams, playing in four championships games during his career. Don caught a touchdown pass in the 1963 game, the club's only championship.

Don returned to Iowa after his playing days. He worked for Blue Cross - Blue Shield and became the owner/publisher of the *Voice of the Hawkeyes* magazine.

NFL Receiving Record

Year	Team	G	REC	YDS	TD
1960	San Diego	14	25	414	5
1961	San Diego	14	47	816	6
1962	San Diego	14	48	771	7
1963	San Diego	7	21	281	1
1964	San Diego	14	49	669	6
1965	San Diego	14	34	485	2
1966	San Diego	14	4	50	0
Career		91	228	3486	27

115 – Lonnie Nielsen

Hometown: Belle Plaine

Nielsen got his start in golf when his father took him to the local course, complete with sand greens. He also learned how to play on grass greens, tying for the runner-up position in the 1970 high school state golf tournament, only to lose in a playoff. He then played for the University of Iowa golf team from 1972 to 1975.

Lonnie debuted on the PGA Tour in 1978 and played full time through the 1983 season. Typically a mid-pack finisher, his best placing came in 1979 with a tie for fifth in the Quad City Open, now the John Deere Classic. His only other top ten finish came in Memphis when he tied for eighth in the Danny Thomas Classic.

In 1984 Nielsen left the tour, becoming the director of golf at Crag Burn Golf Club in East Aurora, New York. As a playing club professional he did very well, winning the 1986, 1987, and 1989 national PGA Club Professional Player of the Year Award. A twelve-time winner of the Western New York PGA Player of the Year award, Lonnie won many regional tournaments. He also won the 1988 PGA Stroke Play Championship and the 1989 PGA Match Play Championship. One of his most satisfying achievements came in 1986 when he tied for eleventh place in the PGA Championship.

There is a saying that life begins at fifty. In the case of Nielsen's golf career, it is true. After turning fifty in June of 2003, he qualified for two Champions Tour events and won two international senior events. After resigning his position at Crag Burn, Lonnie played twenty-six events during the 2004 Champions Tour. He cashed a check in each event, finishing in thirty-sixth place on the official money list. While that was a good year, he needed to earn exemption for the 2005 Tour in the qualifying tournament. A ninth place finish in the six-day event secured his playing card.

One of the tour's longer hitters, Nielsen finished tenth in driving distance while playing twenty-four events in 2005. Lonnie's top performance was a tie for second place and on the season finished in the top thirty golfers on the money list. With that finish he earned full exemption status for the 2006 Champions season and had a career best finish when he lost in playoff in the Jen-Weld Tradition.

116 – Craig Oppel

Hometown: West Des Moines

As a junior at Valley High School in West Des Moines, Oppel was invited to attend the 1984 Olympic swimming trials. He would be competing for a spot on the Olympic team against the country's finest swimmers. Unknown to all except the swimming community, Craig had been a multiple winner in national age-level competition, specializing in the freestyle and butterfly strokes while swimming for the Des Moines Aquatic Club under the tutelage of former Olympic gold medalist, Mike Burton. He competed in the 100, 200, and 400-meter freestyle events during the trials with an eleventh place finish in the 100 as his best. Another chance at Olympic glory would come in four years.

After the trials, Craig added more age-level national championships and began preparing for his senior season. The Valley team had won the state championship in 1984, with Craig claiming individual titles in the 50-meter and 100-meter freestyle. While the team did not repeat the win, Craig won three more individual titles, bringing his career total to seven. His time in the 200-meter freestyle of 1:36.36 set an Iowa and national record. The national record lasted for six years and remains the fourth best of all-time. The Iowa record still stands, as does his record of 49.13 in the 100-meter butterfly.

As a three-time high school All-American, Oppel was highly recruited by the top collegiate swimming schools. Craig chose to attend UCLA because they were a perennial swimming power and offered the best educational program in his chosen field. Swimming in six events each year at the NCAA meets, he placed high enough to be named All-American twenty-one times. In 1985 the U.S. national team participated in the World University games where Craig swam a leg on the 400-meter and 800-meter relays that won gold medals.

Craig's second Olympic opportunity came in 1988. He swam in three events at the trials, making the finals in the 200-meter freestyle. A fifth place finish in the race secured a berth on the U.S. 800-meter relay team at the Seoul Games. With some of the world's top swimmers on the team, the Americans blazed to a victory. Craig became the first native Iowan to win an Olympic swimming gold medal.

117 – Tim Dwight

Hometown: Iowa City

Tim was one of the most electrifying athletes in the history of Iowa high school sports. As a running back for City High in Iowa City he rushed for over 4,000 yards and scored eighty touchdowns. An All-American by numerous publications, Tim was named the Missouri Valley Conference Player of the Year. In both his junior and senior seasons he was first team All-State. Tim also excelled as a sprinter on the track team. Twice he was named the Gatorade Iowa Track Athlete of the Year and won twelve state titles, ten Drake Relays titles and fifteen Missouri Valley titles. As a team, City High won three consecutive state track championships.

Choosing to play football with the Hawkeyes, Tim was in a battle for playing time in the backfield, he even volunteered to be on kickoff teams and play defensive back. Then as a sophomore he was moved to wide receiver. He led the team in receiving three years and left as Iowa's all-time leader in pass reception yardage and receiving touchdowns. As a return specialist with the ability to get to full speed quickly and avoid would-be tacklers, Tim was always a threat to break a long run. As a senior he led the nation in yards per punt return average and was named an All-American.

Drafted in the fourth round by the Atlanta Falcons, Tim opened his NFL career with much of the same flare he showed at Iowa. In Super Bowl XXX he returned a kick ninety-four yards for a touchdown. After three seasons in Atlanta, Tim was traded to San Diego where he became a part of their receiver corp. Injuries restricted his play, and in his final year with the Chargers he was used only to return kicks. Released in 2005, Tim signed with the Patriots as a receiver and return specialist.

NFL Rushing / Receiving Record

8 Seasons	G	ATT	YDS	TD	REC	YDS	TD
Career	101	49	340	3	171	2754	17

118 – Ricky Davis

Hometown: Davenport

At Davenport North Ricky led the team to the 1997 championship. *Parade Magazine* named him fourth team high school All-America and he was named first team All-State. In his one year at the University of Iowa, Davis set a freshman scoring record with 464 points. He earned honorable mention All-Big Ten honors and was selected as a Freshman All-American by *Basketball Times*.

An early entry in the 1998 draft, Ricky was a first round pick of the Charlotte Hornets. He showed promise during his rookie season including a thirty-two point performance in his only starting role. Playing time diminished during year two, and he was traded to Miami. After playing only seven games in 2000-01, he was sent to the Cleveland Cavaliers in a three-team trade.

The Cavaliers were not very good so Ricky was one of their better players, but he earned a reputation as a selfish player with a divisive attitude. He was the team's leading scorer, but when LeBron James became a Cavalier in 2003 Ricky was on his way out. After twenty-two games the trade was made that brought him to Boston.

When Davis arrived in Boston his image in NBA circles was that of a self centered player. He began the season in the Celtics starting lineup then after seven games was moved a reserve. Coach Doc Rivers needed someone to be the leader of the second unit and Ricky was selected. Many doubted he would accept the change or possibly cause problems. Instead, he relished the challenge, averaging sixteen points per game and finished second in the voting for the NBA's Sixth Man Award.

During the 2005-06 season the Celtics were looking for more scoring and although he had done everything asked of him, Ricky was a part of a seven-player trade that sent him to Minnesota. He played the final thirty-six games with the Timberwolves, averaging 19.1 points.

NBA Record

8 Seasons	G	FG	3P	FT	RB	AST	PTS
Career	501	2676	274	1392	1765	1644	7018

119 – Sage Rosenfels

Hometown: Maquoketa

To first see Rosenfels one wouldn't think him to be as athletic as he is. At Maquoketa High School he was named to All-State teams in football, basketball, and baseball. After passing for 1,122 yards and ten touchdowns as a senior, *Street and Smith's* magazine named him one of the top quarterbacks in the nation. As a defensive back he had a three-interception game and also handled the team's placekicking and punting duties. He was a three-year starter on the basketball team averaging twenty points, twelve rebounds, and seven assists his senior season. He batted over .400 his junior and senior baseball seasons playing shortstop and pitching. The number one player on the tennis team, he complied a 40-6 career record. He ran track as a senior, qualifying for the state meet in the 800-meter and 1,600-meter relays.

During a red-shirt year at Iowa State, Sage was voted Scout Team MVP, then spent two years as the backup quarterback before becoming the starter in the 1999 season. After a 4-7 record in 1999, the 2000 season was one of Iowa State's best. They completed the regular season with an 8-3 record and then recorded the Cyclone's first-ever bowl victory, a 37-29 win over Pittsburgh in the Insight.com Bowl. On the season Rosenfels completed 172 of 333 passes for 2,298 yards and eight touchdowns and rushed for 381 yards and ten touchdowns.

Drafted by the Redskins, Sage spent one season in Washington as the third quarterback without playing any regular season games. A trade to Miami produced little playing time. In four seasons he appeared in only thirteen games, two as a starter. His best NFL game came in a reserve role in 2005 when he led the Dolphins to a victory, overcoming a seventeen point second half deficit.

NFL Passing Record

5 Seasons	G	ATT	CMP	YDS	TD	INT
Career	13	109	54	776	6	6

120 – Doreen Wilber

Hometown: Jefferson

Doreen was born in Rutland and moved to Jefferson as a sixth grader. After graduation she married Paul "Skeeter" Wilber, and they made their home in Jefferson. Skeeter repaired cars and once received an archery bow in lieu of payment. Giving it a try, the couple enjoyed the sport and soon began competitive shooting at the Coon Valley Archery Club in Guthrie Center.

To succeed in competitive archery, one must be able to focus on the target and block out distractions. It also helps to forget a poor shot. Doreen had these capabilities and improved steadily. She won her first state tournament in 1962 and eventually became a four-time national tournament champion.

In 1969 Doreen participated in her first world championship. After a slow start, she finished strong but fell ten points short of victory. The 1971 meet held in York, England, was a tune-up of sorts for the 1972 Olympics. Emma Gaptchenko of Russia won by nine points, giving Wilber her second silver medal. Winning the 1971 U.S. Nationals, Doreen qualified for the Olympic games and was the strongest member of the American team.

The Olympic archery event is comprised of two rounds. Each day the archers shoot a series of arrows from four distances; the winner is the person with the highest two-day total. A notoriously slow starter, Doreen was tied for fourth place after the first day, scoring 1,198 and trailing by twenty-six points. Increasing her focus, she tallied a second round score of 1,226, the highest score of either round. With a total of 2,424 points she avenged her earlier loss to Gaptchenko, established a world record, and won the gold medal.

She won the U.S. nationals in 1973 and 1974, along with a fifth place finish at the 1973 world championship. With little left to accomplish, Doreen semi-retired from competitive archery. She continued to go to a few tournaments, more interested in getting together with old friends than the actual competition.

121 – Al Feuerbach

Hometown: Preston

A Preston High School graduate in 1966, Feuerbach was an unlikely candidate to become a world record-holder in the shot put. As a senior he won both the shot and discus at the state meet, but at 6' 1" and 180 pounds he was small for an aspiring world-class thrower. One intangible in the making of an athlete is desire, and Al was prepared to take the necessary measures to accomplish his goal.

Step one was to select a college. Late in his senior season at a meet in Des Moines, Feuerbach met Phil Delavan, a former Iowa State shot-putter that was coaching at Emporia State in Kansas. Al liked what he heard and decided it was the place for him. Step two was for Al to increase his body size. Many weight man used substances, such as steroids, to add bulk to their frame, but not Al Feuerbach. His method was all-natural, a high calorie diet including steak and plenty of milk.

At Emporia State he concentrated on the shot, perfecting his technique and gaining body size. He became the NAIA outdoor Champion in 1967 and 1970 along with indoor championships in 1969 and 1970. After graduation Al was able to devote his full attention to the shot. It paid dividends when in 1971 he set a world indoor record, tossing the shot 68' 11". In 1973 he set the outdoor record of 71'7" that stood for over two years.

Participation in the Olympics is the goal for track and field athletes and Al was no different. He qualified for three different games. At Munich in 1972, he finished fifth, only six and a half inches from the gold medal. It was disheartening but Al set his sights on the Montreal games in 1976. Considered one of the favorites for a medal, he experienced one of his poorer performances as he only threw 67'5", finishing a disappointing fourth. He last chance at an Olympic medal was lost when the United States boycotted the 1980 games.

A five-time winner at the Drake Relays, Feuerbach won four national championships in six years and a Pan Am title in 1971. As the injuries came more frequently and took longer to heal, Al bid farewell to competition in 1983.

122 – Kent Ferguson

Hometown: Cedar Rapids

"Sure I wish I'd made the Olympics. But hey, I'm a kid from Iowa, and because of diving I've seen the world. I'm not complaining. " *USA Today* quoted Ferguson on May 2, 1988, as he expressed these sentiments after a second near miss for membership on the U.S. Olympic diving team. In 1992 the Olympic dream came true with a berth on the three-meter diving team for the Barcelona Games and also the honor of being named the U.S. Male Diver of the Year,

In the 1976 Hawkeye Junior Invitational, he placed third in the one-meter competition and won the three-meter. At the National Juniors in 1977, Kent took home fifth place in the one-meter springboard, his first recognition at the national level. Diving for Cedar Rapids' Washington High School he won conference championships and state titles. He still holds the Mississippi Valley Conference one-meter points record. In 1989, the Iowa High School Swim Coaches Association honored Kent with induction into its Hall of Fame.

Highly recruited, Kent chose to attend the University of Michigan to continue diving. Michigan had one of the top programs and this was a great place for him to pursue collegiate and Olympic aspirations. In 1984 Ferguson won the NCAA three-meter springboard championship. During his college days and through the mid 1990s, Kent was a member of the United Stares diving team, competing in meets throughout the year.

Career Accomplishments

1989 - U.S. Outdoor 3-meter Springboard Champion
1989 - U.S. Indoor 3-meter Springboard Champion
1989 - Olympic Festival 3-meter Springboard Champion
1990 - Goodwill Games, silver medal
1991 - World Champion on the 3-meter board
1991 - Pan American Games 3-meter Champion
1992 - Olympic games fifth place 3-meter finish
1995 - National Outdoor 3-meter Champion
1995 - Olympic Festival 3-meter Springboard Champion

123 – Mace Brown

Hometown: North English

Mace was in professional baseball for nearly sixty years as a pitcher, coach, and scout. He didn't have an opportunity to play high school baseball, as North English did not field a team, so in the summers he played with the town team. Mace possessed a strong arm and also used it to throw the javelin for his high school track team. He attended the University of Iowa on a track scholarship, but after the baseball coach got a glimpse of his ability, he soon became a baseball player.

He first played as a catcher and then switched positions before his junior year to become one of Iowa's top pitchers. After accepting money as a semi-pro player in 1929, the Big Ten declared him ineligible. With his college career over, Mace signed with the St. Louis Cardinals. He spent five seasons in the minors before the Pittsburgh Pirates signed him to a major league contract. During his rookie season, he witnessed the last three home runs of Babe Ruth's career. Entering the dugout after the third dinger, Ruth took a seat on the bench next to an awe-struck Brown.

Mace was one of the first pitchers to specialize as a reliever, starting only fifty-five of 387 career games. His best season came in 1938 when he was the league leader in appearances. He posted fifteen wins in relief and added five saves, making the All-Star team and garnered enough MVP votes to finish ninth.

Brown was with Brooklyn in 1941 and then was purchased by the Boston Red Sox in 1942. In 1943 he again led the league in appearances and also games finished. After two years in the U.S. Navy, Mace returned to Boston for his final season in 1946. He only pitched in eighteen regular season games, but the Sox made it to the World Series where he pitched in one game. After three years as a Red Sox coach, Mace was a scout for Boston until 1990.

Major League Pitching Record

10 Seasons	W	L	G	SV	IP	H	ER	ERA
Career	76	57	387	48	1075.3	1125	414	3.46

124 – Ross Verba

Hometown: West Des Moines

A prep star at West Des Moines Dowling High School, Verba was named 1992 *Parade* All-American and Iowa's "Player of the Year." Highly recruited, Ross chose Iowa over national power Nebraska. He began his collegiate career as a tight end; then in the third game of his red-shirt freshmen season, he moved to tackle. His mobility was average for a tight end, but exceptional as a tackle. He became the starting left tackle in game six and was a fixture throughout his career.

Drafted in 1997 by the Green Bay Packers with the final pick of round one, Ross was headed for the reigning Super Bowl champs, a team in need of help in the offensive line. The talk was that when the season opened the name Verba would be in the starting lineup. However, when preseason camp opened, Ross had yet to be signed and held out until just prior to the final preseason game. The holdout cost him the chance to compete for a starting position and when the season opened he was a backup, playing on special teams. Then due to injuries he had a chance to start, made the most of the chance, and became the regular left tackle. He did an exceptional job, solidifying the offensive line as the Packers marched through the playoffs to the Super Bowl.

After four years with the Packers, Ross signed as a free agent with the Cleveland Browns. The Browns offensive line was comprised of younger players and Ross was a steadying influence. In his first season with Cleveland, he played twelve games at left guard before moving to tackle for the final four games. Ross missed the entire 2003 season when he tore a bicep muscle during the final preseason game. In 2004 he was the only Brown's offensive lineman to start all sixteen games, but a contract dispute led to his release prior to the 2005 season.

NFL Game Record

1997 GB: 16 G **1998** GB: 16 G **1999** GB:11 G **2000** GB: 16 G
2001 Cle: 16 G **2002** Cle: 16 G **2003** Cle: INJ **2004** Cle: 16 G
Career: 107 G

125 – Elmer Layden

Hometown: Davenport

Davenport High School has produced many outstanding athletes, but none have gained more post high school acclaim than Elmer Layden. He was the fullback in the most famous of all collegiate backfields, "The Four Horsemen of Notre Dame." Playing for the legendary coach Knute Rockne from 1922 to 1924, the four backfield members were nicknamed by one of America's most well-known sportswriters, Grantland Rice. In both 1923 and 1924 Elmer was selected as an All-American.

At Davenport, Layden excelled in all sports. He was almost a one-man track team, an All-State basketball player on a state championship team, and of course, an All-State quarterback. Receiving little attention from in-state universities, including the University of Iowa, prompted his selection of Notre Dame.

After graduation from Notre Dame, Elmer became the football coach at Columbia College (now Loras) in Dubuque for three seasons. During the years he was at Columbia, Elmer was able to earn his law degree and pass the Iowa Bar Exam. As was the case with many college coaches at that time, Layden moonlighted as a professional football player. In 1925 the Rock Island Independents paid Elmer $1,500 for a single game, an unheard of sum for a player during that time.

The next coaching stop was at Duquesne University in Pittsburgh for seven years before he went back to Notre Dame as the head coach. For seven seasons he coached the Irish and left with a record of forty-seven wins, thirteen loses and three ties.

In 1941 Layden was selected to be the first commissioner of the National Football League. The game of professional football was gaining popularity and the league needed leadership. As the war began there were struggles by many of the league's teams and Layden had to try to keep the league from ceasing operations. Through the troubling times, Elmer had to weigh his decisions between what he considered best for the league's growth and the directions the owners desired. After five years in the post, the owners decided to make a change and did not renew his contract. Thus Layden's football career ended.

126 – Ben Crain

Hometown: Sloan

It could be argued that Crain, born in Sloan, is the greatest all-around athlete the state has produced. He was a top notch semi-pro baseball pitcher, starred on high school and AAU basketball teams, was a top level volleyball player on national AAU tournament teams, played college football and soccer, shot golf in the low seventies, and is a Hall of Fame softball pitcher.

After the family moved to Sioux City in 1921, Ben began to develop his softball pitching ability and by age thirteen led the Sioux City Warfields to the city title. At the time, softball was the nation's most popular participation sport because of economics; it was cheaper than baseball. Good pitchers were coveted and Crain was able to pitch on a variety of teams throughout his high school days.

Moving to Omaha in 1931, Ben played basketball for one of the top teams in the area. After a year he enrolled at Montana State College playing football and soccer. Missing the excitement of softball, he returned to Omaha. In 1933 the International Softball Championship was held at the Chicago World's Fair. Crain's pitching led the Barnsdall Ramblers of Council Bluffs to the championship. The 1934 Ramblers continued their dominance, compiling a 116-9 record.

As mentioned earlier, Ben excelled in other sports. He played basketball for traveling teams, including a top-rated team from Wisconsin. Several semipro baseball teams in Minnesota employed his services as a pitcher. He not only pitched softball well, but he was also a good hitter. A career .376 hitter, he totaled more than 300 homeruns during his career in the Omaha Metro League.

During his illustrious career Ben pitched more than 100 no-hit, no-run games. He appeared in nine other national tournaments, toiling for a number of teams. There were times when he would pitch the first game of a doubleheader right-handed and the second using his left. He once pitched his team to a championship while supported by a crutch due to broken bones in his foot. In 1976 Ben was elected to the Amateur Softball Association of America Hall of Fame.

127 – Jeff Clement

Hometown: Marshalltown

The nation's attention was focused on two Iowa high school baseball players in the summer of 2002. Clement and Winterset's James Peterson were in a battle to overtake the high school national record for career home runs. With updates almost daily, the state and nation followed the duel until season's end when Clement established the new record with seventy-five, two more than Peterson. Jeff earned All-America honors and was featured in the September 16, 2002, issue of *Sports Illustrated* as part of the "For the Love of the Game" article.

Jeff grew up playing baseball with a talented group of players. In 1996 the Marshalltown team advanced to the Little League World Series in Williamsport, Pa. As high school seniors, they won the 2002 state championship. The Minnesota Twins selected Jeff in the twelfth round of the 2002 amateur draft. Instead of turning professional, he accepted a scholarship offer from the University of Southern California.

During his three years at USC Jeff was the Trojan's starting catcher. He opened eyes immediately by leading the team in home runs, was named Collegiate Baseball Freshman National Co-Player of the Year and Pac-10 Conference Freshman of the Year. Draft eligible after his junior year, Jeff left as a three time All-Pac Ten selection, earned 2005 Baseball America All-America First Team, was a finalist for the 2005 Golden Spikes Award, and was the winner of the Coleman Company Johnny Bench Award as the top collegiate catcher.

During the summers of 2003 and 2004, Jeff was a member of the U.S. National Team. The 2004 team won the gold medal at the FISU II World University Baseball Championships in Taiwan with Jeff hitting a game winning grand slam in the semi-final. Later he was named the Most Valuable Player for Team USA during the thirty-third Annual USA versus Japan Collegiate All-Star Series in Japan.

Draft day 2005 brought great anticipation for Jeff as he was projected to be a first round selection. Once the draft began, he didn't wait long to hear his name called as the Seattle Mariners made him the third overall choice. Jeff played thirty-four games in the minor leagues during 2005, belting six home runs. After promotion to the Triple A level in 2006 it looks as if his dream of playing major league baseball has a good chance of happening.

128 – Kyle Korver

Hometown: Pella

Kyle was born in Lakewood, California, but moved to Pella as a sixth grade student. He developed a passion for basketball on a playground in California and his passion continued through his high school days at Pella High. He began as a reserve on the freshman team and grew into a varsity starter his sophomore year, helping the team to a runner-up finish at the state tournament. As a junior he was selected first team All-State and the Little Dutch returned to state finishing fourth. First team All-State recognition came again in his senior year but not many division one scholarship offers. Of the four he received, none from the Iowa schools, he chose to play for Creighton University.

His career as a Blue Jay paralleled that of his high school days; he was a reserve his freshman season but then became a starter as a sophomore. With his pure shooting mechanics and ability to shoot the three-point shot, he became one of the top scoring threats in the conference. The main cog in teams that qualified for four NCAA tournaments berths, he led the team in scoring during two seasons. Kyle was selected second team All-American and was the Missouri Valley Conference Player of the Year in 2002 and 2003.

Drafted by the New Jersey Nets, he was soon purchased by the Philadelphia 76ers. With long range shooting ability, Kyle acquired the nickname “Sniper” from his teammates. He was invited to participate in the three-point contest during two All-Star weekends, finishing fourth and second. He led the NBA with 226 made three-pointers during the 2004-05 season, and was third in three-point attempts. He has been active in charity work in the Philadelphia area, sponsoring a coat drive that collected 1,500 coats for needy individuals.

NBA Record

Year	Team	G	FG	3P	FT	RB	AST	PTS
2003-04	PHI	74	115	81	19	111	40	330
2004-05	PHI	82	317	226	82	379	182	942
2005-06	PHI	82	327	184	101	270	163	939
Career		238	759	491	202	760	385	2211

129 – Robert Gallery

Hometown: Masonville

Robert Gallery came to the University of Iowa as a 240-pound first team All-State end and left as a 320-pound consensus All-American Outland Trophy winner. Following a red-shirt season, he began 2000 as a backup at tight end, and then injuries on the offensive line forced a switch to tackle. The Hawkeyes compiled a twenty-one and five record and back-to-back top ten rankings during Robert's final two seasons. Much of the team's success is due to the offensive line led by Gallery. He displayed exceptional pass-blocking ability and many times "pan-caked" the opponent on running plays.

From an interior lineman's perspective, the Outland Trophy is on the same level as the Heisman Trophy. This award was established to recognize the best college lineman and Gallery was a runaway winner. He was selected as the Big Ten's 2003 Offensive Lineman of the Year and an unanimous All-League selection by the Big Ten coaches. Robert ended his career with a streak of starting forty-four consecutive games, the longest in the Big Ten among offensive linemen at that time.

On draft day 2004, the wait for his name to be called was short. The Oakland Raiders chose him with the second overall selection. All football pundits expect him to be the mainstay of the Raiders line at left tackle. After subbing at right tackle in the first half of game one his rookie season, he settled in as the starter on the right side.

Not just a "big moose," Robert placed second in the high jump at the Class 1A state meet as a junior for East Buchanan High School, but football was his strength. As a high school receiver Gallery had thirty-three catches for 604 yards and three touchdowns. As a defensive lineman he had career totals of eighty-six solo tackles and ninety assists, with three recovered fumbles and two interceptions. Robert also excelled in classroom. He was named to the Academic All-State football team and was a member of the National Honor Society.

NFL Game Record

2004 Oak: 16 G **2005** Oak: 16 G **Career**: 32 G

130 – Christine Thorburn

Hometown: Eldridge

Christine Thorburn began her sports career as a junior high runner in track and cross country. Born in Davenport, she attended Pleasant Valley Community High School. In cross country she qualified for the state meet in 1984, finishing in the top ten.

Grinnell College was the next stop on her academic road. She ran during her years at Grinnell, but academics were the priority. After graduation in 1992, Christine attended medical school at Stanford University. A knee injury prevented her from running, so she substituted cycling as a means of exercise. Sensing she was fairly fast as a cyclist, Christine joined the Stanford Collegiate Road Cycling Racing Team through the encouragement of a classmate. As a member of the squad, she helped her teammate win the overall individual title and Stanford secure a second place finish in the team competition at the 1998 Collegiate National Championships.

After graduating in 1999, Christine took a break from competitive cycling and spent the next two years as an internal medicine resident. As a postdoctoral fellow in rheumatology at Stanford in 2001, there was more time for Christine to resume competitive cycling. Knee surgery in 2002 cut short her season, but she came back in 2003 to earn a spot on the 2003 World Championship Road Team.

Entering the 2004 national women's cycling elite time trial championship, Christine was a huge underdog to make the Olympic team. She finished the twenty-four kilometer course in 34:16, eight seconds better than the second place cyclist. The victory gave her an automatic nomination to the three-woman squad to Athens. Christine had an impressive performance in her Olympic debut. She finished ninth in the road race and fourth in the time trial, just twenty seconds short of winning a medal.

The 2004 season was a breakthrough season for Christine as she won the Cascade Cycling Classic and was third at the Redlands Bicycle Classic and Sea Otter Classic Stage Race. Internationally she raced in the World Championships in Verona, Italy, finishing seventh in the Team Trial. She added a multiple victories in 2005 and 2006, most notable the Greater Montreal Tour in 2006.

131 – Duke Slater

Hometown: Clinton

The son of a minister, Slater was born in Normal, Illinois, but later moved to Clinton were he attended high school. He chose to attend the University of Iowa to play football and pursue a degree. Fred is considered one of the greatest of all the Hawkeyes, anchoring the offensive line as the school achieved national prominence. He was voted by the fans to the All-Time team and was elected to the Helms Foundation Hall of Fame. This lineman was a three-time All-Big Ten first team selection, a second team All-American in 1919, and then first team selection in 1921. Fred was named to a national college sports writers All-Time All-American squad in 1946.

Fred was one of the first African-Americans to play professional football. At the time the league was in flux with teams surviving for just a few seasons and then folding because of financial difficulties. He began his career in 1922 with the Rock Island Independents. In 1926 he moved to the Milwaukee Badgers, playing there only for one year before the team folded. He then finished his career with the Chicago Cardinals from 1927 to 1931, a dominant two-way tackle on mediocre teams. One of the more impressive aspects of Slater's career was that none of the early black players played as long as Fred. In 1927 he was the only black player on an NFL roster. Fred also played exhibition games with the Chicago BlackHawks, an all-black team that played white teams in the Chicago area and on the West Coast.

During the off seasons, Slater returned to Iowa to complete a law degree, eventually becoming a judge in the Chicago area. He was one of five starters on the 1921 Iowa squad that became lawyers.

NFL Game Record

1922 RI: 7 G
1922 Mil: 2 G
1923 RI: 8 G, 1 XP
1924 RI: 8 G
1925 RI: 11 G
1926 ChiC: 2 G
1927 ChiC: 11 G
1928 ChiC: 6 G
1929 ChiC: 13 G, 1 Int, 1 TD
1930 ChiC: 13 G
1931 ChiC: 9 G
Career: 90 G, 1 Int, 1 TD, 1 XP

132 – Keith Molesworth

Hometown: Albia

As a high school student Keith was too small to be competitive in sports. A growth spurt after graduation allowed him to be successful at the college level. At Monmouth College, Molesworth earned twelve varsity letters in four sports. His talents in baseball and football allowed him to play professionally in both sports. During the years he played football for the Chicago Bears, Keith also played professional baseball, rising as high as the Triple A level.

In 1928 and 1929, he was both player and backfield coach for the Portsmouth Spartans, the franchise that became the Detroit Lions. In 1930, he played for the Ironton Tanks before signing with the Bears. In Chicago he led the offense as T-formation quarterback in a backfield that included Red Grange and Bronko Nagurski. Defensively he was a back that could stop ball carriers with punishing blows. The Bears also used him as a punt returner since he had exceptional speed.

Following retirement as a player, Keith stayed involved with football through coaching. He spent eight years at the US Naval Academy and then six more coaching minor league football. In 1952 he entered the NFL ranks when he signed on with the Pittsburgh Steelers as a backfield coach. In 1953 he became the first coach of the Baltimore Colts. After a 3-9 season, Keith moved to the front office. Until his death in 1966, Keith was vice president and director of player personnel. The first draft he oversaw yielded twelve players that became regulars for Baltimore. Those selections helped lay the foundation for the Colts becoming NFL champions in only six years.

NFL Record

		Running			Receiving		
7 Seasons	G	ATT	YDS	TD	REC	YDS	TD
Career	81	348	1105	8	35	464	2

		Passing				
7 Seasons	G	ATT	CMP	YDS	TD	INT
Career	81	226	86	1486	18	19

133 – Jim Kelly

Hometown: Fonda

There are times in life when an expected event leads to a change in one's life. This happened in 1917 to army engineer Jim Kelly. Walking near a practice field when a football came rolling his direction, Kelly kicked the ball back to the students. They were in need of a coach and before long Jim filled the role. That was the impetus leading this Iowan to the position as head coach of the 1956 Olympic track team.

Kelly was born on a farm near Fonda. He was a back in football, played basketball, and ran the hurdles and middle distances for the track team. He scored seventy-five points in a 102-2 basketball victory during the 1912-13 season. Jim attended Buena Vista College for a year, transferred to Morningside until injured in football, and then transferred to the University of South Dakota until entering the service. After his time in the service, Kelly finished his degree at South Dakota.

After graduation from USD in 1920, Kelly accepted a coaching position at Fonda. In a two-year stretch the Fonda football team only lost one game while playing the likes of Fort Dodge and Mason City. He also coached basketball and other sports as needed. His next coaching stop was at Buena Vista before moving to DePaul where he coached the football, basketball, and baseball teams. The 1933-1934 school year saw each of the teams complete undefeated seasons.

When the Minnesota Gophers offered a track position, Jim took the job to focus on just one sport. Always experimenting with new techniques, he changed the footwork and spin of the discus throwers, leading to world records by two of his athletes. In 1948 his team was a piecemeal group that scraped their way to a National Collegiate title.

After serving as coach during the 1951 Pan Am Games, Kelly was selected to coach the 1956 Olympic track team. He wildly boasted the team would win twelve gold medals. Some scoffed when he held the trials in June for the late November games citing the team would be out of shape. Every move Jim made was right and the team exceeded expectations, bringing home fifteen gold. Had that football not bounced his way, the United States possibly would have missed one of track's greatest coaches.

134 – Debbie Esser

Hometown: Woodbine

Debbie's first attempt as a seventh grade hurdler ended with both she and the hurdle on the ground. The next season she found her stride; to be exact she found three strides. In an AAU meet she took three steps between hurdles while others took four. From that time on she dominated the hurdle races. At the conclusion of her career at Woodbine High she had won thirteen state titles, a record that still stands. She was a four-time champion in the 100-yard hurdles and 220-yard low hurdles. Other titles came in the long jump and as a member of the mile-relay team that set a national record. Debbie also ran cross-country and played basketball, helping the team to the state tournament.

Before entering Iowa State, she ran in the national 400-meter hurdle race, winning in record time. As a Cyclone she specialized in the 400 hurdles, becoming the first woman to win four AIAW titles in the same event. A nine-time All-American for ISU, she was elected to the Cyclone Hall of Fame in 1998.

Each spring the Drake Relays invite some of the world's top athletes to compete in special events. Esser was one such individual, and in front of stands full of fellow Iowans she came away with 400-meter hurdle titles in four different Relays, 1977-79 and 1982.

Training at Texas A&M after graduation from Iowa State, she participated in national and international meets. She was the United States' only representative at the 1979 World Cup, finishing third behind runners from East Germany and the Soviet Union. In a meet in Germany she won the 400-meter hurdles and was selected as Athlete of the Meet. At the height of the Cold War she ran in a meet in Russia with national pride on the line. The story is that after she drew lane one, an oversize hurdle was placed in the lane, throwing off her timing. Whether true or not, Esser brushed the hurdle leading to a narrow defeat. Respect comes in various ways; if the story is true, it is evident the amount of respect opponents had for her ability.

Debbie credits much of her hurdling success to her life growing up on the farm. Helping with the daily chores, walking beans, baling hay, and other tasks helped keep her in shape. Today it would be referred as cross training, then it was a way of life in Iowa.

135 – Corkey Nydle

Hometown: Ottumwa

As one visualizes the swing of a golf champion, it would likely have a smooth arc and flow into a high finish. Corkey Nydle did not have a swing resembling that picture. While she did not have the most technical swing, she was able to fashion accurate shots with her irons. Her strength was in the short game, displaying an uncanny ability to get the ball close to the hole. Her greatest attribute was her attitude. She was able to shrug off a bad shot and move on to the next.

After graduating from Ottumwa High School, Corkey attended Stephens College in Columbia, Missouri. Her advisor at Stephens was Ann Casey Johnstone, a native of Mason City and one of the top amateur golfers in the country. In 1953 the State Amateur was match play format and Corkey made the finals. The opponent was Ann Johnstone and Nydle defeated her mentor in the thirty-six hole match.

Her career was nearly derailed in 1969 when doctors diagnosed an ailment in her hand as radiation poisoning. Told she would likely lose the hand, Corkey responded by exercising the hand through squeezing a rubber ball. A year later she won her fifth state title. In 1972 she overcame an elbow injury to win her sixth title, tying Johnstone for most in a career. She added four runner-up finishes and had a string of twenty-four state championship play top ten finishes. In 1988 the inaugural class of the Iowa Golf Hall of Fame was chosen and Corkey was the only female elected.

Nydle's competitive record speaks for itself, but devotion to helping young golfers and promoting golf in the state makes her rise above others. She served on the USGA Junior Girl's Committee and thirty years on the Iowa Women's Golf Association, including a term as president. Corkey has taken players to the national junior tournament and helped organize junior tournaments in the state. One of the tournaments is named in her honor.

In spite of her commitments she has played in a variety of age-level events. Still possessing a competitive spirit, she collected eleven senior women's titles. She has also been a member of the Iowa team in USGA Women's State Team Championship play.

136 – Bing Miller

Hometown: Vinton

When he was sixteen, Vinton native Miller pitched for the hometown team called the Cinders. His father had been a minor league ball player and two of his brothers played for the Cinders. Possessing a strong arm, teams were seeking his services. In 1914 he entered the professional ranks pitching for the Central Association team in Clinton. In his three-year stint in the Association, a position change was necessary due to an arm injury that brought an end to his pitching career. With an ability to hit, he was too valuable to cut loose, so he was converted to an outfielder.

After spending 1918 overseas in the military service, Bing returned to baseball in the Southern Association. In 1921 both Pittsburgh and Washington claimed Miller; at that point Commissioner Landis decided in favor of Washington. Thus Miller made his debut with the Senators only to be traded to the Philadelphia Athletics after one season.

Bing played eleven seasons for the A's, with a year and half interruption when he played with the St. Louis Browns. On his 1929 return to Philadelphia, the team was loaded with talent, playing in the World Series three consecutive years. In the 1929 Series, the A's had a three game to one lead but trailed 2-0 going into the bottom of the ninth. After scoring two runs to force a tie, Al Simmons doubled; Jimmy Foxx was intentionally walked bringing Miller to the plate. On a two-strike count, Bing slammed a single to right field sending Simmons home with the series-winning run.

Miller and the A's won the series in 1930 and then lost to the Cardinals in 1931. In 1935 the Red Sox organization purchased Bing's contract and he played his final two seasons in Boston. After retiring from the playing field, Bing spent eighteen years coaching in the majors with Boston, Chicago, Detroit, and Philadelphia.

Major League Batting Record

16 Seasons	G	AB	R	H	2B	3B	HR	RBI	BA
Career	1821	6212	946	1936	389	96	117	990	.312

137 – Eddie Watt

Hometown: Iowa City

Eddie was born in Lamoni but went to school at Iowa City High. As a pitcher for City High, Watt struck out a record fifteen batters in the 1959 state baseball championship game. Despite his heroics the team lost the championship to Thomas Jefferson High School of Council Bluffs. Eddie's 1959 season was brilliant; in the 98.2 innings he pitched, he had an ERA of 0.56 and 206 strikeouts. He threw three ho-hitters, two coming back to back in the tournament. The second included nineteen strikeouts in the substate final against Fairfield.

After two years at UNI, Watt signed with the Baltimore Orioles playing for Fox City in 1962. Eddie spent four years in the minor leagues and duplicated a high school fete, pitching back-to-back no-hitters. In 1966 he made the major league roster with Baltimore.

After thirteen starts and a record of 2-5, Watt was relegated to the bullpen. Manager Earl Weaver employed a bullpen-by-committee strategy and Eddie was a valuable component. Once in the pen he finished the year with a 7-2 record and four saves. That season the Orioles won the franchise's first World Championship. His best year came in 1969, when he was 5-2 with a career-high sixteen saves. In his eight seasons with Baltimore, he pitched in three different World Series, compiling a 0-3 record with a 4.06 ERA.

Known as a prankster, Watt and a teammate once painted the Kansas City bullpen in the Orioles' colors: orange and black. In 1974 he played for the Phillies and in 1975 finished his major league career with the Cubs. For two years Eddie played as an independent in San Diego's farm system and then became a minor league manager for the Padres. Eddie later served as pitching coach in the Houston Astros and Philadelphia Phillies minor league systems. He has also coached at various levels in the Braves organization.

Major League Pitching Record

10 Seasons	W	L	G	SV	IP	H	ER	ERA
Career	38	36	411	80	659.7	530	213	2.91

138 – Bob Allen

Hometown: Des Moines

After the bombing of Pearl Harbor, Des Moines native Bob Allen enlisted in the Army Air Corps. Serving as a gunnery instructor, Allen was able to practice a sport he enjoyed, trap shooting. At the time the Army was disposing hundreds of thousands of shotgun shells and clay targets. Bob received permission to use the supplies and he had plenty of time and material to practice. Spending countless hours on the range, he became proficient to the point of breaking 400 straight targets.

Following his discharge, Allen went to Monte Carlo entering a few shooting tournaments. Things didn't go quite as planned; he wasn't winning. After taking a little time off, his shooting came together and the wins started to come. Bob was able to parlay his winnings into a business venture. With ideas originating during his time in the service, he put into place the beginning of his world-known Bob Allen Gun Club Sportswear Company. Today the company provides a full line of shooting apparel to shooting enthusiasts worldwide.

When the company wasn't consuming his time, he was entering shooting events. During the late 1940's and early 1950's, Allen was one of the world's best shooters. Bob won his first All-Around Iowa State championship in 1948. He followed as the All-Around national titlist the following year and then five more times in a nine-year span. On the international scene he won tournaments in numerous countries, including the 1949 clay tournament in Havana, Cuba. He also was a member of the record breaking United States four-man shooting team.

Athletes in other sports can make a mistake yet overcome it to claim victory. One mistake in trap shooting and you are likely out of the competition. It is difficult enough to hit one moving target, Bob's specialty was doubles, breaking two simultaneously released targets. His list of championships could go on for pages, but most impressive would be the thirteen All-American awards, the pinnacle for shooters. Elected to virtually every shooting hall of fame, Bob "Shooter" Allen's legend lives on though he was tragically killed in an automobile accident in near Omaha in 2004.

139 – Jack Fleck

Hometown: Davenport

Fleck pulled off one of sport's greatest upsets. In the 1955 United States Golf Open, the immortal Ben Hogan was poised to claim an unprecedented fifth title. Finishing early, Hogan was in the clubhouse with the lead when talk began of an unknown Iowan making a charge with a run of birdies. Fleck finished his round of sixty-seven with a seven-foot birdie putt on hole number eighteen to force a playoff with Hogan. The playoff featured a legend of golf that had won everything against a part-time tour player that had not won anything. Everyone expected the pressure to be too much for Fleck, causing him to fold. Jack did not fold; instead he continued his brilliance to win the eighteen-hole playoff by three strokes.

Jack caught the golf bug as a caddie during his younger days in Davenport. He played four years of golf for Davenport High School and after graduation in 1939 turned professional. His first employment was as an assistant at the Des Moines Golf and Country Club. After serving in the military during World War II, Fleck came back to Des Moines only to have the clubhouse destroyed by fire leaving him without a job. With few options available, Jack moved back to Davenport and accepted a position as the club pro at two municipal courses.

He was holding that position when he began his first summer on the PGA Tour in 1955. When they teed it off at the Open, Jack had played in only fifteen tournaments, with his best finish being eighth. When one observes the history of both golfers, it makes Fleck's upset of Hogan all the more unlikely.

The next few years after the Open championship, Jack continued to play on the tour and worked as a club pro with stops in Michigan, Illinois, and California. He had wins at the 1960 Phoenix Open and the 1961 Bakersfield Open. He had a chance to win a second U.S. Open. In 1960 he was leading with six holes remaining, but a three-putt doomed him to finish third, losing to an upcoming young pro named Arnold Palmer and an amateur by the name of Jack Nicklaus. The 1963 season was Fleck's last on the tour. He has played at a few Senior events over the years, in particular the Senior PGA Championship.

140 – Bill Koll

Hometown: Fort Dodge

As a junior at Fort Dodge High School, Bill Koll did not win a single wrestling match. Surprisingly, he was back out as a senior. In a complete reversal, he didn't lose a match in 1941 in route to the 135 pound high school state championship. The Dodger team also claimed the state championship.

Drafted into the Army during his sophomore year at Iowa State Teachers College (UNI), Koll earned a military Bronze Star for his participation in the Battle of the Bulge and D-Day. Back on campus in 1946, Bill continued his unbeaten streak winning the NCAA championship. His junior and senior seasons were more of the same, unbeaten and national champion. In both the 1947 and 1948 tournaments Bill was selected as the meet's Outstanding Wrestler, the first to win multiple awards. So dominant as a collegian he was taken down only once and was reversed just twice. He capped his brilliant career by pinning all five of his opponents at the 1948 NCAA meet

Koll won a berth on the 1948 U.S. Olympic team by winning the 147.5 pound freestyle weight division and he was named the Outstanding Wrestler. In the London Olympics he suffered defeat for the first time in eight years as he placed fifth.

Bill began a career as a wrestling coach in 1948 at the University of Chicago. Coming back to Iowa, he was hired by Cornell College in 1951. When UNI's Dave McCuskey retired in 1952, Koll was selected as his replacement. In addition to coaching wrestling, he also coached tennis, assisted in football, and taught physical education. Bill led the team to a fourth place finish at the NCAA Championships in his first year and compiled a 71-42-6 record during his twelve years at the UNI helm. He left in 1964 to become the coach at Penn State, where his record was 127-22-7 in fourteen seasons. Six times his team finished in the top ten at the NCAA meet, and he had three wrestlers win individual NCAA national championships.

He has been named to the National Wrestling Hall of Fame, the Helms Athletic Foundation Wrestling Hall of Fame, the Pennsylvania Wrestling Hall of Fame, and the Iowa Wrestling Hall of Fame.

141 – Kevin Ritz

Hometown: Bloomfield

Born in Eatontown, New Jersey, Kevin moved to Bloomfield as a youngster and attended Davis County High School. A high school all-star as a senior pitcher, he completed one of the all-time best season-earned run averages with a 0.70 mark over fifty-three innings. Kevin then played baseball for Indian Hills Community College in Centerville for two seasons before the Detroit Tigers selected him in round four of the 1985 amateur draft. Before signing a professional contract, Kevin played with the Alaska Panhandlers in the Alaska summer league for college players.

His first professional experience came in 1986 at Gastonia. He worked his way up the Tigers chain, including a stop at Glen Falls, where he led the team in innings pitched and wins. Kevin was brought up to the Tigers mid-season of 1989 and made his major league debut on the fifteenth of July. A bright spot on a poor Tiger staff, Ritz was voted the team's Rookie of the Year.

After four injury-plagued seasons in Detroit, Kevin was selected by the Colorado Rockies in the 1992 expansion draft. An arm injury delayed his start in Colorado until 1994. After pitching only fifteen games the first season, he pitched well in 1995 and started game one of the playoffs against the Atlanta Braves. Kevin had his best year in 1996, winning a club-record seventeen games before recurring arms problems forced him into retirement.

Major League Pitching Record

Year	Team	W	L	G	SV	IP	H	ER	ERA
1989	DET	4	6	12	0	74.0	75	36	4.38
1990	DET	0	4	4	0	7.3	14	9	11.05
1991	DET	0	3	11	0	15.3	17	20	11.74
1992	DET	2	5	23	0	80.3	88	50	5.6
1994	COL	5	6	15	0	73.7	88	46	5.62
1995	COL	11	11	31	2	173.3	171	81	4.21
1996	COL	17	11	35	0	213.0	236	125	5.28
1997	COL	6	8	18	0	107.3	142	70	5.87
1998	COL	0	2	2	0	9.0	17	11	11.0
Career		45	56	151	2	2753.3	848	448	5.35

142 – James Jones

Hometown: Davenport

Playing only two games his senior season at Davenport Central High School because of a broken leg probably hurt Jones' chance to get a scholarship from a Division I school even though he was a two time All-Conference performer. The coaches at UNI were intuitive enough to give him a chance and it paid dividends for both. Jones provided them with outstanding defensive line play, which led to his being the Cleveland Browns' third round selection in 1991. From the mid-point of his freshmen year, Jones was a defensive starter for the Panthers, playing at defensive end until his senior season when he was moved to linebacker. James was recognized for his achievement by being named All-Gateway twice and All-American first team as a senior.

He became a starter at defensive tackle for the Browns in his rookie season. During his first season James totaled fifty-one tackles including one sack, three fumble recoveries, and one interception that he returned for a twenty-yard touchdown. In four seasons with the Browns, Jones was called upon to be a blocking back in short yardage situations. He scored a rushing touchdown and caught a touchdown pass. While in Cleveland, James became very involved with charity work and was named the Browns " Edge NFL Man of the Year."

Jones played with the Denver Broncos in 1995, and then spent three seasons with the Baltimore Ravens. He finished his playing days with the Lions in 1999 and 2000.

NFL Defensive Record

Year	Team	G	TKL	INT	SKS	FF	FR	TD
1991	Cleveland	16	51	1	1.0	0	3	1
1992	Cleveland	16	45	0	4.0	0	1	1
1993	Cleveland	16	39	0	6.0	0	0	1
1994	Cleveland	16	30	0	3.0	1	2	0
1995	Denver	16	31	0	1.0	0	2	0
1996	Baltimore	16	37	0	1.0	0	0	1
1997	Baltimore	16	52	0	6.0	3	0	0
1098	Baltimore	16	55	0	5.5	1	1	0
1999	Detroit	16	48	0	7.0	4	0	0
2000	Detroit	16	45	0	3.5	2	0	0
Career		160	433	1	38.0	4	9	4

143 – Denise Long

Hometown: Whitten

With the advent of ESPN and other sports channels, fans now see many exciting basketball games each year. But one of the most thrilling games was played in 1968 during the Iowa Girls Tournament. Long's Union-Whitten team scored a dramatic 113-107 overtime championship game victory over Everly. The tournament was a showcase for Denise as she scored a state-tournament record ninety-three points in the first round game and a record 282 points in four games.

Some believe the "golden era" of Iowa high school girls basketball was from the late fifties to the early seventies. If that is accurate then Denise Long is the poster girl. Others scored more points during their career, but none can match her legend. In 1965 she came onto the high school basketball scene scoring 920 points as a freshman. Each succeeding year her point total increased to finish with 6,250 for her four-year career, at the time a national record. Her senior year point total of 1,986 and per-game average of 68.5 are six-player records.

With the good, there usually comes some bad. The championship game with Everly came in Denise's junior year, so during the state tournament run in 1969 Union-Whitten was expected to repeat. The country was aware of Iowa girls basketball through television coverage and an article in *Sports Illustrated.* The article featured Long and her teammates as they prepared for the 1969 tournament. In the semi-final the bad happened; Union-Whitten was upset by Allison-Bristow. Denise always put team achievements above her own. The loss was devastating, only to be followed by a loss in the consolation game. This was an unfortunate ending to the career of Iowa's "Queen" of basketball.

Later that spring she was the first woman ever drafted by the National Basketball Association. The San Francisco Warriors made the selection, and while she didn't play in the NBA, she did play in the first attempt at a professional women's league. She also played on an United States amateur team that toured the Orient in 1973. In 1979 Denise played one game with the Iowa Cornets. She scored one point in forty seconds of playing time and received a standing ovation as her playing career ended.

144 – Tony Baker

Hometown: Burlington

When no NFL team drafted him following his Iowa State career, Baker spent the 1967 season playing for the Des Moines Warriors in the Professional League of America. At the time it was a type of minor league. Tony was the league's leading rusher and signed with the New Orleans Saints as a free agent.

In his first pre-season with New Orleans he played very well, but his season ended when he suffered a shoulder separation in the first game of the regular season. The 1969 season was much better for Tony, earning a trip to the Pro Bowl. His average gain per carry of 4.9 yards led the NFL as he totaled 642 yards on 134 carries.

After four games of the 1971 season Tony was traded to Philadelphia, spending the year and a half with the Eagles. He next played with the Rams for two seasons, and then to San Diego for one season to finish his career. Throughout his years in the NFL Tony played mainly as a reserve and was often called on to block, but he did rush for 2,087 career yards.

After football Baker moved to Omaha. Tragically he died in an automobile accident near Monticello. He had been back to attend his thirty-fifth class reunion at Burlington. Iowa will remember Tony as a tremendous athlete for the Greyhounds, participating in football, basketball and track. As a fullback he earned second team All-State laurels in 1962 and held the school high-hurdle record for many years.

NFL Rushing and Receiving Record

Year	Team	G	ATT	YDS	TD	REC	YDS	TD
1968	New Orleans	1	4	2	0	0	0	0
1969	New Orleans	14	134	642	1	34	352	1
1970	New Orleans	8	82	337	1	12	47	0
1971	New Orleans	4	29	125	0	6	44	1
1971	Philadelphia	5	17	49	0	4	36	0
1972	Philadelphia	13	90	322	0	16	114	0
1973	LA Rams	14	85	344	7	0	0	0
1974	LA Rams	14	53	135	5	46	51	0
1975	San Diego	13	42	131	1	6	27	0
Career		86	536	2087	15	82	685	2

Bibliography

Books

Carroll, Bob [et al.] editors *Total Football: The Official Encyclopedia of the National Football League* New York: Harper Collins Publishers 1997

Clark, Jerry E. *Anson to Zuber: Iowa Boys in the Major Leagues* Omaha, NE: Making History 1992

Couppee, Al *One Magic Year, 1939, An Ironman Remembers* N.P. 1989

Feinstein, John *The Punch: One Night, Two Lives, and the Fight That Changed Basketball Forever* New York, NY: Little, Brown & Company: 2002

Feller, Bob. *Strikeout Story* New York: Bantam Books 1948

Hennings, Chad. *It Takes Commitment* Sisters, Oregon: Multnomah Publishers 1997

Layden, Elmer. *It Was a Different Game* Englewood Cliffs, New Jersey: Prentice Hall 1969

Offenberger, Chuck *Bernie Saggau & the Iowa Boys* Madison, Wisconsin N&K Publishing 2005

Paup, Bryce. *What's Important Now* Sisters, Oregon: Multnomah Publishers 1997

Stevens, Todd. *Cyclones Handbook* Wichita, Kansas: Wichita Eagle and Beacon Publishing 1996

Wolfe, Rich. *Kurt Warner, And the Last Shall be First* Chicago, IL: Triumph Books 2002

Warner, Kurt. *All Things Possible* New York: Harper Collins Publishers 2000

Des Moines Register Hall of Fame Induction Articles

Brown, Rick

Den Herder's work ethic paid off in NFL career; 07/17/1988

Winning, not cash, was Kimball's reward; 08/03/1997

Burns, Jane

Daytona drama fueled Lund's career; 07/15/1990

Hansen, Marc

Esser does three-step, hurdles into Hall of Fame; 07/28/1991

Harman, Susan

Corkey Nydle has enriched Iowa golf for five decades; 07/24/1994

Lehmer, Larry
Hilgenberg: First family of Iowa linemen has first hall of famer in Wally; 04/19/1987
Logue, Andrew
Boddicker baffled even the best hitters; 08/13/2000
Hawkeye star lives out his dream in Canada; 08/04/2002
Roby, Nichols beat the odds; 08/24/2003
Housh, Leighton
Iowa Hall of Fame Adds Power Hitter Hal Trosky; 04/04/1965
Maly, Ron
Ex-Yankee hurler Pipgras into 'Hall'; 04/11/1976
'72 Olympic golf medalist Wilber into Register 'Hall'; 04/05/1981
Ex-Chief Podolak to Register's Hall of Fame; 04/20/1986
Ex-Brave Dittmer in Register Sports Hall of Fame; 07/10/1988
Schallau and tennis: A match point; 07/14/1996
McCool, Dan
Successful wrestler, coach; 07/07/1996
McGrane, Bert
Berwanger, Devine, Kinnick, Layden, Slater; 03/18/1951
Pick Wier, McConnell, Beisser; 03/25/1951
Anson, Clarke, Faber, Feller; 4/15/1951
Select Gotch, Burns, Whitney; 04/15/1951
Olympic Track Champs Carr, Saling, Taylor Named; 04/22/1951
Lynn King, Johnny Armstrong in Hall of Fame Both Pint-Sized Gridders; 05/06/1951
Vance Famed For Strikeouts; 04/07/1952
Bancroft in Hall of Fame: Sioux Cityan in big time for 19 years; 03/28/1954
Ex-Cyclone Glen Brand joins 'Hall'; 04/07/1957
Coggeshall joins Sports Hall of Fame; 03/22/1959
'Hall Niche to Bing Miller, Hero of '29 World Series; 03/26/1961
Joe Laws' Grid Feats Earn Berth in 'Hall'; 04/02/1961
Severeid in Iowa Hall of Fame; 03/25/1962
Anderson is chosen for Iowa 'Hall'; 04/01/1962
Whitehill in Iowa's 'Hall'; Rapids Pitcher Won 218; 03/24/1963
Olson, Jeff
'Shooter' Allen is truly a shooting star; 07/21/1996
Peterson, Randy
'Lefty' Joe Hatten: Truly a hometown hero in Bancroft; 07/25/1993
Craig broke the mold for running backs; 07/26/1998
A career beyond his wildest dreams; 07/25/1999
Turnbull, Buck
Thompson Into Iowa Hall of Fame;03/26/1967
Grid Coach Shaw in Iowa 'Hall';03/22/1970
Glassgow Added to 'Hall'; 04/01/1973
Doran's rise: from college 'B' team to NFL kings; 03/31/1974
Mann first woman to enter Iowa 'Hall'; 04/06/1975
Olympian Smith joins Register's 'Hall'; 04/01/1979
From Waterloo to Dallas to Register Hall of Fame; 03/30/1980
Iowa Wrestling Coach Gable joins Register's Hall of Fame; 03/29/1981
Koll named to Register's Sports Hall; 04/14/1985

Preston's Feuerbach persevered to take his shot; 07/16/1989
Westphal, David
Marathon swimmer Nelson joins Register Hall of Fame; 04/11/1982
White, Maury
Kelly Added to Register's Hall of Fame; 03/30/1969
Jack Fleck Goes Into 'Hall' on 1955 Open Shocker; 04/02/1972
'Cinch' pick Duncan enters Hall of Fame; 04/04/1976
14-time national diving champion Olsen named to Register's 'Hall'; 03/26/1978
Crain made pitch as one of best softball players; 07/02/1989
Big talent grows in small package; 07/01/1990

Personal Interviews / Correspondence

Casey Blake, Judy Collison, Billy Cundiff, Tim Dwight, Mike Eischeid, Cal Eldred, Jim Fanning, Bob Feller, Joel Hilgenberg, Mark Hillebrand, Ken Janvrin, Ron Juffer, Mark Kacmarynski, Gerald Leeman, Bonnie Meier, Bob Oldis, Craig Oppel, Doreen Wilber, Paul Wilber, Jamie Williams

Internet Websites

Adams, Amy "Thorburn's competitive spirit pushes her to pedal for medal in Olympics" <http://med.stanford.edu/spotlight/archive/christne_thorburn.html>
Albom, Mitch "When nobody knew what a Heisman was" <jewishworldreview.com/0701/albom071001.asp>
Barnett, Bob "1936: The First Draft" <www.footballresearch.com/articlesfrpage.cfm?topic=1stdraft>
Barnett, Bob "Massacre in Cincinnati" <www.footballresearch.com/articlesfrpage.cfm?topic=massacre
Dimitry, Steve "Extinct Leagues" <www.geocities/colosseum/Arena/6925wb/.html>
Dougherty, Bill "A Short History of Baseball in Batavia" www.muckdogs.com/frame_pages/team_history.htm
Nichols, Bill "Machine Gun Molly hopes there will always be a WBL" <www.lkwdpl.prg/nworth/molly.htm>
Puma, Mike "Gable dominated as wrestler and coach" <www.espngo.com/classic/biography/Gable_Dan.html>
Schonwald, Josh "Jay Berwanger, first winner of the Heisman Trophy" < www-news.uchicago.edu/releases/02/020627.berwanger.shtml>

Baseball Reference <baseball-reference.com>
Bob Feller <bobfeller.com>
Carolyn Nichols Tennis Home Page <carolynnichols.com/Rankings/2000/page4.html>
Central College Athletics <central.edu/athletics/football/records/rushingrecords.html>
Dan Gable <dangable.com>
Des Moines Buccaneers <bucshockey.org/95-96/clemmensen.html>
Drake University <drakebulldogs.org/track/natashakaiser-brown.php>
Drake Relays <drakerelays.org/relays/athleteshalloffame.htm>
Drake Relays <drakerelays.org/Kruger.html>

Drake Relays <drakerelays.org/release25.htm>
Free UK <jezbrown.freeuk.com/column6.htm
Green Bay Packers <packers.com/gameday/1939/1270/htm>
Grinnell College Athletics <Grinnell.edu/offices/ce/newa/080920041>
Hockey Goalies <hockeygoalies.com/bio/clemmensen.html>
Historic Baseball <historicbaseball.com/players/baker_gene.html
Iowa Association of Track Officials <iatfcc.org/?TF%/20Girls%20Records.html>
International Basketball <ibasket.it/news/news.phtml?id=35>
Iowa Golf Hall of Fame <iowagolf.org/HTML/Homepage/halloffame.htm>
International Swim Hall of Fame <ishof.org/imarshof1979.htm>
Korver, Kyle Creighton University <creighton.edu/~KeK03412/aboutme.html>
Ladies Professional Golf Association <lpga.com/player_results.aspx?id=400>
Matt Bullard <mattbullard.com>
Minnesota Vikings <Vikings.com/frontoffice_detail_objectname_jerry_reichow.html>
Molly Bolin <mollybolin.com>
Mt. San Antonio College <vm.mtsac.edu/relays/HallFame/Feuerbach.html>
National Trapshooting Hall of Fame <traphof.org/inductees/allen_bob.htm>
NCAA <d3track.cpm/HallofFame?Main.htm#Kip_Janvrin>
Negro League Baseball Players Association <nlbpa.com/baker_gene.html>
NFL Players.com <playersinc.com/players/playerid.aspx?id=25000>
Northern Baseball League <northernleague.com>
PGA Tour <pgatour.com/players/bio/460187>
PGA Tour <pgatour.com/players/intro/460012>
Professional Disc Golf Association <pdga.com/tournament/players/num=7438>
Professional Disc Golf Association <pdga.com/playerprofiles/julianakorver.php>
Quick Stats <qkstats.net/mside/track/2001/trackresults.html>
SI.com <cnnsi.com/events/1996/Olympics/storyolympics/ol>
The Mat & USA Wrestling <themat.com/athletebio/pressdetail.asp?aid=12590>
The Mat & USA Wrestling <themat.com/athletebios/asp?id=12590>
The Valley <mvcstats.org/reporting/indoorTrack_mens.asp>
Tiny Lund <tinylund.com>
University of Michigan <umich.edu/~bhl/hhl/olup2?ol1992.htm>
USA Basketball <usabasketball.com/history/mpag_1959.html>
USA Cycling <usacycling.org/bios/user/bio. php?id=26>
USA Track and Field <usatf.org/athletes/bios/2002/Little_Kevin.asp>
USA Track and Field <usatf.org/athletes/bios/Kruger_AG.asp>
USA Track and Field <usatf.org/athletes/bios/oldbios/janvrin.asp>
USA Track and Field <usatf.org/athletes/bios/oldbios/Kaiser.asp>
USA Track and Field <usatf.org/athletes/bios/Woody_Joey.asp>
USA Track and Field <usatf.org/athletes/hof/morgantaylor_frederick.asp>
US Olympic Team <usoc.org/26_22213.htm>
UT Chattanooga <gomocs.com/article.asp?articleid=34049>
Wikipedia <en.wikipedia.org/wki/George_Saling>
Wikipedia <en.wikipedia.org/wki/Morgan_Taylor>

Image Credits

Arena Football League, Des Moines Register, Major League Baseball. National Basketball Association, National Football League, National Hockey League, tinylund.com, Craig Oppel, U.S. Olympic Committee, Professional Golfers Association, Ladies Professional Golfers Association, Professional Disc Golf Association, University of Iowa, Iowa State University, Drake University, University of Northern Iowa, Stanley Warner, Virginia Tech University, Topps Card Company, Upper Deck Card Company